THE INTENTIONAL FAMILY

THE INTENTIONAL FAMILY

Jo
Carr
and
Imogene
Sorley

ABINGDON PRESS
Nashville
New York

THE INTENTIONAL FAMILY

Copyright © 1971 by Abingdon Press

ISBN 0-687-19112-2

Library of Congress Catalog Card Number: 71-158668

SET UP, PRINTED, AND BOUND BY THE
PARTHENON PRESS, AT NASHVILLE,
TENNESSEE, UNITED STATES OF AMERICA

To
Mother, and Mother, and Gana
and in grateful memory of
Daddy, and Tommy, and Dad

Contents

Chapter One

The Intentional Family?

Families come in a variety of packages. Intergenerational. Multilingual. Bichromatic.

Some families have eleven kids.

Some have no kids.

Some have grandparents and a resident aunt.

Some have only one parent.

Some have only one person.

Some are rich, some poor, some middlin'.

But we all come in a frustrating combination of two life-styles—at times *intentional*, at other times *otherwise*.

The two mind-sets are poles apart.

The otherwise family meanders through life, falling into a vocation, happening into a pattern of days, chancing upon a way of life. It is uncommitted.

The intentional family, though, has done some basic thinking about who it is and where it is going. Having looked at the whole of life, as much as is possible, it moves out into the world, progressively deciding its pattern, building structures for its days, embracing its way of life. It is becoming committed.

The intentional family learns the agony of having looked deep into life to see things as they really are—and is acutely aware of how little it can do about them. But it knows, too, the occasional moment of exultant joy at having worked through to the solution of *some* problems; and it knows the real comradeship of participation in the fellowship of the concerned.

The otherwise family, not having seen, knows neither the agony nor the ecstasy.

The intentional family is aware of itself and of its potential for growth in wisdom and joy. It seeks to be aware of each of its members, to be conscious of them as persons. It keeps itself in creative tension, mutually teaching and learning, mutually giving and receiving.

The otherwise family is unaware of its own identity, and unwilling to investigate its own potential.

The intentional family sees life more nearly as a whole, and all of it interrelated. A household is able to function because of a community, city, state, nation, world—all of which contribute to its daily well-being, and to each of which it owes its own contribution. It is a part of the past, a participant in the present, and a protagonist of the future. The history of mankind and the geography of the world come together to make this moment, like the sands in the neck of the hourglass, and must cascade out now into the future of the family of man.

The otherwise family sees today, and experiences only its own little orbit from home—to office —to school—*ad oblivion.*

The intentional family asks deep questions, and searches—really searches—for answers.

It is possible to drive through East Anywhere, right into the heart of a deteriorating slum, and not *see* it. It is also possible to see, and to sorrow —and never ask the basic questions of how it came to be a slum, and why. Not asking hard questions means not finding valid answers. So we turn away sorrowing, and the slum remains. Only the intentional among us pry and persevere, and go to City Hall and the Board of Realtors and the editorial page, asking hard questions and demanding honest answers, and thereby making things happen.

The alternate choice is to ask no questions at all. It keeps one uninvolved.

It is also possible to drive through West Anywhere, right into the heart of modern suburbia, and not *see* it, not be aware of closed doors and insulated loneliness. What are the basic questions about creating community here—and what are the answers?

Asking no questions keeps one uninvolved.

The intentional family participates in movements toward social justice, lending the weight of its vote, its legwork, its purse, its muscle, and its focused mind. Or it initiates problem-solving structures where honest study reveals a need.

The otherwise family sits.

The family which *chooses* to live, learns from the *hard* saints of history.

"Soft saints" have soft hearts, but sometimes they tend to have soft heads as well. "Hard" saints have compassionate hearts, but they have steel girders in the mind. They are committed not to a bed of roses, but to a task; and there is no room in the task force for those whose souls are fat or whose minds are full of weeds.

The intentional family is open to change, ready to re-evaluate, and, if need be, to make a new model. The otherwise family, having found its rut, tends to become rigidly molded to its confining contours.

The intentional family is conscious; the otherwise family is unconscious. The intentional family lives on behalf of all mankind; the otherwise family lives on behalf of itself.

No family is going to be intentional in all situations. But this must be the goal. To aim for less is to belittle the possibilities. We will continue to be a frustrating combination of both life-styles. But the only responsible option for the concerned family is deliberately and continually to make the intentional choice.

The decision is ours.

We make it deliberately, or we make it by default.

But we make it.

All of which sounds quite formidable. That part which is most difficult to express is the *joie de vivre*—that keen joy in living—that comes with the conscious expenditure of our irretrievable days. To compare those moments of worth with ordinary living is like comparing the drab browns of daguerreotype with living color.

Chapter Two

Within this House

We are what we are because of relationships.

Women can understand themselves as women only in terms of their relationship to men. This is obvious—if there were no men, what would be unique about women? The counterside of the coin is equally true—a man is a man because of the complementary nature of women.

Parents *are,* because of children.

Children are free to be children, only because of parents. (Remember *Lord of the Flies?* Ralph and Piggy no longer had that privilege.)

So we are what we are because of relationships.

Within the family there is one relationship that is basic to all the others. That one was undertaken voluntarily:

She and I—Him and Me

A number of gifts at the wedding shower were marked "His" and "Hers"—stitched into towels, embroidered on pillowcases, even painted on coffee mugs. Then he opened the bulky gift from an old army buddy. It was a blanket—olive drab, like ten thousand others of government issue—and boldly lettered "US."

Marriage is a partnership. It is the first and basic relationship within the family. And it is first and basically a matter of mutual acceptance.

Most of us fall in love with and marry that certain someone because he—or she—is so different. "I never knew *anyone* like him before." "She is so . . . unique!"

Then the first thing we do *after* marriage is set about trying to remake that person to be just like ourselves. Hold the phone! Stop the remodeling! *Accept,* and rejoice in, the uniqueness of the other. Until we do, we are (1) frustrated, because we can't change him, or (2) undone, because we *have* changed him from that which we loved in the first place.

Maybe the marriage ceremony itself ought to be reworded: "*Accept,* love, honor, and cherish." Or perhaps the word honor includes acceptance. Either way, it is the basic premise upon which a marriage is founded.

Helen listened to the beauty shop harpies run down their husbands. She knew none of them, but she could not help feeling belittled, as well as indignant. "It just isn't cricket," she said later. "Anybody who has offered to take on your support, *for the rest of your life,* must have liked you a great deal. It really isn't cricket to run him down!" A question of loyalty is involved.

This most personal partnership is based in part on trust and acceptance. You love each other as you are. This is the one person before whom you can stand naked, baring your deepest yearnings, revealing your most glorious dreams, confiding your most devastating mistakes. And you are still accepted.

When you have really been cut down to size by the outside world over some stupid blunder about which you would just as soon not tell anyone, you can share it with this one who loves and accepts you anyway. And in his acceptance you can find it possible to accept your own inadequacies.

> Marriage is a partnership—but it is made of *two individuals.* Each is a person, and each has a right to—and an obligation to—continue to exist as a person. Each must honor this right.

. . . together you shall be . . .
But let there be spaces in your togetherness,
And let the winds of the heavens dance between you.
Love one another, but make not a bond of love:
Let it rather be a moving sea between the shores
   of your souls.[1]

[1] Kahlil Gibran, *The Prophet* (New York: Knopf, 1923).

Tread gently into another's private moment. Or tread not at all. There are times when you must wait to be invited in. It is important to honor the bounds of privacy, willing to *not* intrude, willing to let another *not* confide.

Just "being there" is not the same thing as "being present" to a situation. The latter implies an awareness, a being alert to the beloved—a sensitivity to his needs.

The intentional marriage partner will "be for her what she needs"—a rock upon which to lean, if what she needs is loaned strength or one who enables her to stand in her own strength, if what she truly needs is supportive confidence.

"I try consciously to provide an atmosphere at home that will preserve him," one wife stated. She is endeavoring to be for her husband what he needs, enabling him to revive at home, to rejuvenate, to become.

Sometimes what he (or she) needs is that which the British refer to most aptly as "Her Majesty's Loyal Opposition." Marriage is one great tension, where each can be for the other a "blessed enemy"—to counter, to question, to provide the temper of another point of view. This loving conflict is a possibility, though, only where mutual acceptance is already established. Only then can a couple disagree creatively. Only then can each be for the other both sounding board and mirror.

"We agreed when we first married that we

would be for each other what the street urchin was for Julius Caesar," a husband explained. "All the way through the play, the ragamuffin speaks to the emperor from somewhere within the crowd —'Hey! Your crown's on crooked!' We do this for each other. It has a stabilizing effect."

But it would not work if there were not first an accepting, and a being accepted.

The alternate attitudes are defensive. What we do to a person whom we are unwilling to accept creates barriers beyond which we are never able to proceed. We become increasingly dishonest— and not-quite-honest—with each other, wearing increasingly more complicated masks, building ever fancier façades. But until we *accept* each other, quite simply, we have not established a relationship in which we are free to be ourselves.

"A good marriage is important to me," stated Irene Harrell. "It's one of the things I hold most dear. It's a lot more important to me than many other things I would also like to have. . . . And I try to remember to live accordingly."

She suggests that we make a list of

"Things I'd Like to Have
my own way
a mink coat
a happy marriage
no ashes on the rug

18

a vacation at the beach
hollandaise sauce on the asparagus
sheets tucked in at the foot of the bed."

Make your own list—it might go on for pages and pages. Then recopy it, putting the most important item at the top, the next most important second, and so on down to the thing you care least about.

"You'll recognize right away that some of the items are incompatible," Mrs. Harrell continues. "Your husband can't stand sheets tucked in at the foot of the bed. So which do you want most —a happy marriage or tucked-in sheets? You can't have them both. Maybe if you were all of six-feet-two, tucked-in sheets would bother you as well. So don't tuck them in; they don't have top priority. Sure, it takes a little longer to get the bed made in the morning 'cause the sheet is all whopper-jawed. But so what? You know what you wanted most, and you're getting it. And a happy marriage is . . . worth giving up a lot more than tucked-in sheets." [2]

We will work at relationships with other people—really work at them. But with this one, we get to feeling that we don't have to bother. "I

[2] Irene Harrell, *Good Marriages Grow* (Waco, Tex.: Word Books, 1968), p. 95.

caught him (or her), so that's settled." There is a certain fine balance between being accepted and being taken for granted. It is good when husband and wife feel sufficiently comfortable with each other that they do not have to work at it all the time. But the smart thing *is* to work at this basic relationship.

There is a quaint quatrain from a children's book:

> It's very very impolite
> To turn off mom and kiss the light.[3]

It becomes less humorous as it becomes more true. No one—not mother or middle child or master of the house—likes to be *turned off*. And no one likes to be so casually regarded.

Us and the Kids

Our offspring, with whom we share a household, are unique. No two of them are alike. No two react in the same way to the same stimulus.

It is one thing to read in a book that children are not alike—even children within the same family. It is easy to give intellectual assent. But somehow it always seems to come as a real shock

[3] Michael Sage and Arnold Spilka, *Dippy Do's and Don'ts* (New York: Viking Press, 1967).

to discover that the second baby is so emphatically *unlike* the first—and the third, nothing at all like either of the other two. (Personal observation notes this is true through the fifth child. Beyond that, only research data available.)

How great! They *are* unique. Unrepeatable.

What a travesty that we spend so much time trying to shove them into the same mold. Molds stifle. And bind.

The creative within each of us needs room to grow—and the intentional family honors and provides for this growth. It regards each of its children in a separate spotlight.

It can seize even the selection of a birthday gift as an opportunity for underlining this uniqueness. A flute would be a marvelous gift for one child. But an old beat-up rattletrap car may be just what another needs. A small boy whose aunt gave him an old clock to dismember, discovered the world of mechanics.

Doug brought home a greasy old carburetor one Saturday morning when he was five. "Where did you get *that?*" I asked.

"Bought it off a Mark," he said, hunkering down beside his prize with a cleaning rag and a tool tray.

"What did you pay for it?" I persisted.

Doug grunted, "Quarter." Doug got a dime a week for allowance, a nickel of which he put in

21

the basket at Sunday school. Just before I blurted
out some ridiculous objection, I got a good look at
Doug's face. Totally absorbed, totally intrigued,
and deeply proud of owning his own *real* carburetor, he fairly oozed contentment. He never
had anything that brought him more pleasure.
He tinkered with it for days—taking apart and
putting together, adjusting and cleaning and oil-
ing, showing its innards to his peers. (And to
think, for four cents more, I would probably have
bought him a color book!)

There is no mold.

Accept

In the intentional family, each child is accepted.
This permits him the freedom to be himself.

Each of us is a person, with gifts to give to
the world that no one else can give. Not one of
us is perfect, but we are each one a human personality. God accepts us as we are, and this gives
us cosmic permision to be ourselves. This does not
give us the right to be slobs or to live at less than
our best. But it does give us the right to self-
acceptance.

Our children, too, are persons of worth, *as
they are now*. Deliver us from thinking, "He'd
be a person of worth, all right, if he'd just quit . . .
or if he'd just start . . . or if he'd just be more like
his Grandad." He is of worth now. And the in-

tentional family accepts each of its members with no strings attached.

It is all right if Tim is tone deaf. He's a born mechanic. It is also all right for Tom to be all thumbs with tools or baseballs. He might be a whiz at physics, if someone helped him discover the fact.

To accept a person is to acknowledge that he, as an individual, is of worth.

Jim's gift to the world is not the same as Paul's, nor is Paul's the same as Cathy's. For Jim is not Paul. He is Jim, and unrepeatable.

Expect

Accepting implies expecting. It means anticipating a worthy contribution. If I accept Jim, as himself, I shall expect from him a Jim's-worth—a full Jim's-worth.

The Barneses have three sons. David, the middle one, marches to a different drumbeat, and lives now in a boarding-school village for mentally retarded children. There he is a contributing member of society, for he works in the school laundry. His mother wrote:

"We are proud, my husband and I, of all our sons. The biggest boy of our house is a fine athlete, the leading track man in his school. The littlest boy is a good student, standing at the top of his class. And the middlest boy of our house—

David—is the very best laundry worker in the village where he lives." [4]

This is what is means to accept. And to expect. *Each* has his worthy contribution.

The day-school class for the educable retarded was planning a Christmas pageant, and two of the mothers were talking about it. One said, "Shelley is going to sing in the angel choir. They've practiced for weeks on 'Away in a Manger.' It's so hard for them, and they are doing such a *good* job!"

The other replied proudly, "Cindy is going to be a story listener. Always, in order to have a story told, you must have story listeners, you know. She recognizes the importance of her part."

This, too, is to accept, and to expect.

No person's contribution is the same as another's. Yet each *has* a contribution. And the intentional family requires of him that he make it.

It behooves a parent not to criticize so much or demand so much that the child must live with guilt or with regret that he has been unable to measure up to parental expectations. Unrealistic demands place a dreadful burden on a child. What should be required of him is the best that he can give, but it is important to have some idea of what that best might be. To judge too harshly

[4] Carole Barnes, "The Middlest Boy of All," *Reader's Digest,* April, 1968, p. 59.

is a renunciation of the child himself. The expectations must be within the framework of the acceptance.

How does a family decide, then, what the expectations can be? Are there clues or guidelines to the capabilities of a particular child? How can we *keep* from making unrealistic demands?

An aid to objectivity may be the simple expedient of trying to look at the child through other eyes. Suppose John were my neighbor Kate's son. How then would I regard his behavior, his attitudes? Would I see him merely as exercising his prerogative to be an individual, or would I read the veiled cry for help in his actions? What would I see if he were Kate's boy?

Most schools give periodic achievement tests to show not only how the child rates in the abilities tested, but also to give some indication of his development. An over-tired child, or one whose family had a real hassle at breakfast, may "blow" a single test—but a series of such evaluations should give some guidelines.

Nothing beats the valid parent-teacher conference when both realize that their common concern is what is best for this child. A mature parent and a mature teacher, neither one on the defensive about "my position," can talk over a child's aptitudes and behavior patterns and give each other real guidance in seeing the child as a whole person—and in meeting his very individual needs.

Pushing too hard? Demanding too much? too little? Perhaps the most important element in realistic expectation is mature parents who are willing to see the child as he really is, and not as a projection of what they wanted him to become.

Enable

How shall the child make his contribution to life? How shall he even recognize what it is he has to offer?

Perhaps he never will, without the intentional assist of his family.

Children need some exposure to a variety of experiences. These may include a summer art class at a community center, or music lessons, or a course in wild life or archaeology offered by the museum. It is hard to pick out a library book for a child, then *make* him read it, and have him appreciate it *anyhow*. But deliberate luring—leaving around the house intriguing books particularly chosen to appeal to his current interests—can entice him into becoming a reader. And then all sorts of doors are open. A gift of a pattern and cloth might be a door-opener for a middle-sized girl.

Is there a local little theater that has a children's group? Are there Scout troops that do all sorts of things? Can the family go visit a taxidermist, or a fish hatchery? Or go to the symphony, or to see a play? These experiences give a child a basis for discovering his own interests.

There is, certainly, the present danger of over-regimenting the lives of children by encouraging their participation in too many structured and organized activities. There are things that we can lead a child into. But allowing him time to discover other interests of his own is another sort of enabling.

Sam wants to collect snakes? Accepted. (On certain conditions, of course. They must be properly cared for. And confined. And not shoved under the noses of those of us who remain wary. And the interest must be genuine.) This being so, the family provides a place for the snakes. And we *all* learn some herpitology. (And it came to pass that Sam found his career in the process. He is now a herpitologist at the Houston Zoo, and travels to Trinidad and Guatamala to collect specimens—just like he used to travel down the farm-to-market road east of town looking for coachwhips and racers and rat snakes.)

Susan studies the stars. So *set* the alarm for the night of the eclipse—and make hot cocoa at two o'clock in the morning. And perhaps route a summer trip to include a visit to an observatory. These times of enabling a child to pursue an interest of his own build choice memories. "Remember the night we . . ." "Remember the time we . . ."

By providing a safe place for the stamp collection, a nook for the easel and oils, we honor the interests (and the uniqueness!) of each member of the family—and we *enable* each to find himself.

Discipline

Every child has the right to a *disciplined parent* —one who knows where he is going and does what is necessary to get there. In such a frame of reference, much petty disciplining becomes unnecessary.

A child who knows what is expected of him, and what the results will be if he does not come through, is saved from the worry of whether or not he is going to *do* his task, and from the worry of whether or not he can get away with skipping it this time. This *frees* him, in a sense that the undisciplined child is never free.

To accept a child does not mean that we must tolerate unacceptable behavior. We do him no favor if we lead him to believe that he can foist himself off on society as a bully, or a baby, or a self-centered prig. He acquires at home the behavior patterns that he will use to confront the outside world. Unless they are reasonable patterns, he is poorly equipped indeed.

One of the most significant things that a growing youngster must acquire is the ability to make decisions. This is not a skill which can be *taught*, but one which must be learned. Practice in decision-making is essential, and each child must be permitted this practice. He must be allowed to choose, to plan, to initiate, and to decide. Some of his assumptions will be false, and some of his conclusions will seem unreasonable to the adult spectator. (His steps were a little wobbly when he was learning to walk, too; and his pronunciation was still amateurish at three, remember?) It is the responsibility of the family to allow each child to make decisions. This means accepting the decisions he makes. If they are wrong ones, he will have to endure the consequences. But we *accept* his decisions, or we say by our unwillingness to do so, "You aren't really a person at all. You can't do any deciding."

Jerri, secretary at a university student center, said one day in awe and shock: "Do you know, parents *make* kids what they are!" She was watching students, some of whom were torn up, confused, and unable to relate to other people. And she was seeing how much of this had been brainwashed into them at home.

Her indictment is not totally true, of course. Every child has some ability to decide whether or not he will *stay* what his parents made him. But it contains so much truth that each of us as parents should stand accused. Are we doing this to our own children? Thwarting, belittling, underselling, rigid-molding? Ignoring them, or babying them, or shoving them aside, bypassing *their* needs and hungers? We stoop to this, quite unconsciously, in order to save time, or in order to maintain our own image.

It is so easy to become embroiled in power struggles with our children. We haggle and nag. We trade privileges for chores, and take them away for transgressions. It keeps us all in a stew just keeping score.

The intentional family can remove itself from these struggles. Having made certain decisions together, it has only to recall those decisions to memory. This becomes an effective example in *self-*discipline.

Launch

A home is a launching pad, of sorts, customized for each of its members.

Accepted at home as a person of worth, the child-now-grown has a confidence in self that enables him to confront whatever life may hold. More than that, it enables him to size up opportunities, and seize the one that he can handle most creatively.

An intentional family readies each of its members for launching. It has been cutting apron strings all along. It has been undergirding his thinking, supporting his decisions, honoring his integrity. Then, "in the fullness of time," it sends him out. He is launched *by* his family, and *for* his family, toward an independently intentional life of his own.

Inter-sibling

No two children have the same heredity. This is an accepted genetic fact.

It is equally true, and not always remembered, that no two of them have the same environment. Only the youngest has *all* the big kids to plague and instruct and chasten and spoil him. Only the eldest has to cope with *all* the little kids. Only the middle one finds himself too big to play in the sprinkler with these, and too little to drive to the swimming pool with those.

These are built-in inequities.

But there are built-in compensations, too.

Camping out is scary, even in the back yard. Unless you've got a big brother. Learning to use makeup is scary, too, and awkward. Unless you've got a big sister. And there is just no cheering section like younger brothers and sister, who *know* you can stake a tent better and fix a toy better than anyone else in the world—who know you are the prettiest, and the smartest, and—the most!

Living under the same roof, though, almost inevitably creates friction. The intentional family will minimize it wherever possible. Honoring the bounds of privacy, for instance, removes a lot of little irritations. This does not mean providing his own room for every child—for that may be neither practical nor wise. It means seeing that little brother doesn't play with the clarinet, and that sister's diary is inviolate. It means *not* going into someone else's dresser drawers. It means observing absolutely the privacy of mail. It means *not* demanding to know after a phone call, "Who was that, and what did he want?"

Paul Tournier tells of a little girl whose mother has been walking to and from school with her each day, and who is now big enough to walk alone. That first day of walking alone is momentous. But when she arrives at home, flushed with her own success, she is greeted by Mother's barrage of questions. She tells a small untruth about her route home—not because she intends to lie, but because she has need of a secret, at least a tiny little secret. "That is exactly what is important; and that is what her mother has not understood; she has indiscreetly plied her with questions in order to learn everything." [5]

Part of honoring the bounds of privacy is a matter of allowing each member of the family to have an identity of his own.

The Family of One

Even the family of one member has a relationship. It can get on its own nerves, creating its own friction until it cannot function—or, in accepting itself, can live fully and contribute significantly.

[5] Tournier, *Secrets* (Richmond: John Knox Press, 1965), p. 7.

Some of the unhappiest people on earth are families of one—the waspish old maid, the crotchety old curmudgeon, the eternally young lady with the desperate, too bright façade, the burned-out bachelor—there are endless variations on the empty-loneliness theme.

But some of the great souls of the world have also been families of one. There is a certain dignity about a person who *copes* with life. There is a greater freedom to place life where it can count the most, when doing so does not also jeopardize a family.

The dedicated and intentional family of one will accept his present status and his foreseeable future honestly. Then he is in a position to make realistic plans for investing his own life.

Acceptance. That seems to be the key.

Unto the Third Generation

Blessed or blasted are those families wherein three generations dwell under the same roof—blessed if they can accept one another, and blasted if they cannot.

They can be of such genuine mutual help! The grandfather who permits the toddler to enjoy the engrossing practice of taking consecutive steps enables the child to walk (and enables his distracted mother to get on with supper). The child, in turn, by his very need, allows Grandfather to be of service.

The grandmother who helps shell peas for the freezer or pick out nutmeats for a cake is *enabled* to be a contributing member of the family. Her presence there with a napping child frees the young mother to run to the grocery store—where she, in turn, can be of help to Grandmother by picking up a skein of yarn while she is gone.

There will be friction, of course, in any intergenerational family. (There is friction in *any* family.) It can become an impassable barrier, or it can be recognized as normal friction.

Much of it can be eliminated by the simple expedient of sitting down together to talk it out. This intentional discussion will need to be both loving and objective. It is better to risk the temporary problem of hurt feelings than to spend the rest of life putting up with a situation that could have been corrected by loving frankness. Irritations need to be *admitted*. Some of them can be ironed out—and that makes the other ones more tolerable.

People are living to be older than ever before. This very fact will make the inter-generational family a more and more familiar pattern. As in *any* relationship, an intentional and thoughtful approach can ease matters for everyone concerned.

The grandparent moving in would usually prefer not to do so. He would rather live the rest of his life independently, and in the comfortable familiarity of his own home. But this option is not always open. Sometimes a rest home is, and sometimes it is not, a wise choice. Admitting that "living with us" is a second best choice, we can accept the situation, make mutual adjustments and concessions—and then proceed, as an expanded family, with the intentional living of our days.

A family needs to be intentional, also, in its relationships to the grandparents who live across town, or across the state or across the nation. It can be a name-only relationship, with an occasional note beginning, "I have really meant to write oftener, but . . ." Or it can be an intentional sharing—of joys and sorrows and recipes and new books and the funny things the youngsters say.

A committee was discussing the date for an all-day meeting. One lady suggested Thursday. "Because," she said, "my husband and his brother always have lunch with their mother on Thursdays." Her husband and his brother are busy fifty-year-old businessmen. What a delightful and intentional way they have found of being present to an elderly mother.

Maybe the situation is that the family does *not* have a grandmother. Ellen and her four- and eight-year-old daughters went to a local nursing home and asked if they might borrow one. They promptly adopted her, went to visit her every week or so—sometimes took her posies out of the garden, or a small plate of cookies. They talked with her about Brownies, and spelling words, and what color to choose for a school dress. And they listened in fascinated awe to stories of coming West in a covered wagon, and camping out every night along the way. They got her recipe for sourdough. And they made some! And of course they took her some sourdough biscuits, with a bit of honey. Each filled a gap in the lives of the other. It was an intentional relationship.

Chapter
Three

Beyond
this
House

*"We are like dwarfs seated on the shoulders of
giants. We see more things than the ancients, and
things more distant . . . but this is not due to our own
stature."* —Bernard de Chartres

We who live in this twentieth century are sitting on the shoulders of the past. We are beholden
to Socrates and Voltaire and Pope John. The
past has lived for us, and lives on in us. And we,
on the wedge-blade of history, have an obligation
to live for future generations.

My family by sheer happenstance was born
into a situation wherein they can have a roof
over their heads, books to read, an opportunity to
go to school. They have enough to eat and sufficient clothes to wear. By happenstance we have
inherited on a silver platter five thousand years of
cultural progress.

In addition to those things which the past has
given us, we have also minds with which to think
and hands with which to do. It would be a
travesty and a disgraceful waste *not* to think and
not to do.

37

All our time will be given—we decide where.

All our money will be given—we decide where.

All our energies will be given. We decide where. The intentional family makes these decisions intelligently and carefully. Then it spends itself until it is weary and frustrated and thrilled to the teeth.

We have just one life to use. We can give it for a cause, or throw it away in front of a truck. *Not* giving it is just another form of throwing it away.

My family, blessed by happenstance of birth, is called by God to give itself on behalf of all mankind.

The future doesn't just happen. It is, rather, *determined* by the actions and attitudes of people. *Someone* is going to determine our future.

Rosa Parks did—she refused to stand up on a bus in Birmingham. "My feet hurt," she said. "I won't stand up." Her decision was the beginning of a revolution in America.

Gandhi did—he said, "I will not get up until you bring me an untouchable, by the hand." His decision was the beginning of a revolution in India.

Ralph Nader, Madeline Murray O'Hair—*persons* determine our future.

The man of faith should understand the world better than anyone else. Then, in the lucidity of this understanding, and in the strength of his faith, he takes valid action.

It is this that made Joan of Arc, who was basically a woman of faith, go fight for France. This is what drove St. Catherine of Siena from contemplation to politics; Florence Nightingale to battle with vermin and dirt and disease; Kagawa to dwell with the inhabitants of Tokyo's slums.

This is what drives the intentional family into active participation in the world.

Relationships go beyond the family group. We are an integral part of a total world community.

Part of a Neighborhood

The old-fashioned neighborhood where people knew and supported each other—what happened to it? Is it gone? Or just neglected? Are we unable to interpret "neighborhood" on the eighth floor of an apartment complex? Do we move so often that we never get acquainted?

Or can neighborhood come to be a *more* significant term because it is intended and worked at?

It was easy to be friendly back in the old-fashioned neighborhood. We all bought bread at the same grocery store; our cough syrup and ice cream cones from the same corner drug store. We all went to the same school, and the same church, and the same Saturday matinee.

Things have changed. Today we must deliberately open some lines of communication with those around us, or they will never exist. There are people who are intentionally establishing neighborhood within an apartment building or in an urban renewal complex. And they do it in order to minister to the needs of others.

Sociologists are saying that mankind's most urgent problem today is loneliness. And loneliness stalks the *un*-neighborhood where people are anonymous and no one cares. The intentional family must lend itself to the community, to fulfill for it whatever needs it can fulfill.

Part of this lies in being aware. We look with seeing eyes, or we do not know that there are any needs.

An awareness of unchanneled boy-hours as the real problem behind an outbreak of vandalism may cause a father to take on the responsibility of a scout troop. An intentional family *enables* him to serve in this way, making available the time in the knowledge that a scout troop, too, can be a redemptive fellowship.

The mother may make herself available to the community through the brewed-to-share pot of coffee. (The coffee klatch can be a blessing or an abomination. It could become a committee of the concerned within the neighborhood. Any one participant could make it so.)

The deliberate investment in a really long telephone cord enables a homemaker, even while she prepares supper or finishes the ironing, to be available to those who call because they need her strength.

Nor does the working woman forfeit her membership in a neighborhood when she becomes employed. Her concerns reach beyond office hours, causing her to stop at the library to pick up an intentionally selected book for a heartsick or lonely or unmotivated neighbor. She may use a lunch hour to renew a meaningful relationship, or to undergird with her own vitality a hospitalized friend. She may find it possible to create neighborhood at the office, or in the teacher's lounge, or at the factory coffee bar.

Through letters we can make ourselves available to an expanded neighborhood. They need not be just the dull and prosaic recital of the week's events; they can be a lending of oneself for the needs of another.

Belonging to a neighborhood involves a responsibility for its physical appearance. Run-downness is catching. If we let a yard deteriorate and the paint peel unnoticed, we belittle the whole block.

Of course the opposite is also true. Once there was a little girl, the true story goes, who was very poor. Her hair was stringy, and her face was perennially dirty. One day, though, her teacher gave her a pinafore. It was white, starched and fresh, and very ruffled.

When the little girl's mother saw it, she washed her daughter's hair, and heated water for a bath. The child looked so fetching that—well, something more seemed required. So the family straightened up the house a bit—and her brother went out and raked the yard—and her Dad nailed back a couple of loose boards on the fence. They even planted some flowers out front.

In the days that followed, Dad walked a little straighter, seemed like. There was a new sense of worthiness in the family that spilled over into everything they did. When the flowers bloomed, they looked so bright and gay that the lady next door was prompted to plant some, too, and to rake her own yard, and to paint her porch. An epidemic of painting and planting and raking and rejuvenating spread through the whole community. Because of a pinafore.

It isn't always so. Sometimes a teacher gives a child a badly needed garment, only to find out later that the father has sold it to buy bay rum.

But *once* there was a little girl . . .

And run-up-ness is catching, too.

A new family moving into the community offers obvious opportunities for neighborliness.

The grandmother who gardens invitingly offers herself and her time to the children of the neighborhood. (To their mothers, too, on occasion.) And the children who take her a plate of warm cookies cement a significant relationship. This same intentional grandmother might teach a cluster of little girls to embroider in a sewing class on summer afternoons. All manner of wisdoms can be divulged during a sewing class.

It is possible to belong to the Ladies' Aid or the P.T.A. or the Lodge because of a speech impediment that renders us incapable of saying "no." But it is also possible to belong intentionally. Or to *become* intentional in a group into which we have merely drifted. One clear-thinking presence in such a group can bring it to account—or to study, or to action.

Mrs. Moore was once a missionary to China. Now she's a missionary to our town. She accomplishes this almost unobtrusively, but she jerks me up, somehow. I am awakened nearly every time I cross her path. She isn't *placid*. In a meeting she *listens*. Then she asks a brief, searching question that underlines a truth or forces an issue. She participates in all manner of going concerns. Intentionally.

In these and in countless other ways the intentional family finds techniques for saying what it has to say, and for creating structures through which it can be what it needs to be to the community.

Saying what it has to say? There are times

when this cannot be done by being gracious and polite.

"Recently, at a dinner party, I listened to a guest's bigoted remarks about a minority group not represented at the table. The host tried skillfully to change the subject, but the guest persisted. Then, glancing at his young children near him, the host said softly, 'Please. Not in my house. I suppose your private attitudes are your business, but when you air them here, they become mine. I have to tell you that I disagree and disapprove. If I didn't speak out now, you—and the children here, and the other guests—might think that my silence is tacit approval. I hope you understand.'" [1]

Dinner was a rather silent affair, and the importunate guest left early, but in taking his stand, the host had made it a worthy evening.

We Are Part of a School District

Education—along with everything else these days—is in revolution. Or it *should* be! The teaching techniques that worked a generation ago have neither the scope nor the intensity to freight the knowledge explosion today.

What are the answers? The intentional family

[1] Evan Hill, "It's *My* Life, Isn't It?" *Reader's Digest,* Oct., 1968, p. 218. Condensed from *Christian Herald.*

will do some homework here, too. Specific brows-
ing among educational periodicals in the library
could be a revelation, giving us some insights
as to what is being done in some school districts.

It might also be revealing for us to find out
what is actually being done in our own school
district.

There are questions—probing and pertinent
questions—that we need to ask locally.

What about the budget? How many thousands
of dollars are about to be spent to refurbish the ad-
ministrative offices? Is this amount in keeping
with the salary teachers are receiving? Does dis-
crepancy here have any bearing on a teacher's
attitude, on how eagerly she approaches her part
of the task? Does the athletic budget compare
realistically with the academic budget? (Are we
better equipped for football than for science labs?)

What about academics? Are the necessary background courses being taught to equip those who
go on to college? What about those who do not?
Is vocational training available? Practical? Updated?

Does our school have a *worthy* course in sex
education? Is it required? Is it taught three grades
too late?

Has the school a library, or access to one? Is
it current? Is there a program for keeping it so?
Are there funds available?

Is there a course in Negro history? (There

should be. This has been a gross omission from American history books.) If we live in an area to which another minority group has been strongly contributive, do we study their history or culture or language? Mexican history and conversational Spanish should be taught in the Southwest, for instance.

What about teachers? Do we challenge our youth to this vocation as one of *real* service and worth? Do *we* honor teachers with our backing and support? What sort of community honor do teachers' salaries reflect? Are schools understaffed? Do we stifle the creative ability of teachers by forcing them to conform to the layman's idea of what educational practices should be?

Is our school segregated? Is there token integration? Are we guilty of token acceptance of other human beings? Where do valid answers lie in *our* community? And are we intentional enough to hunt them out?

If we work hard enough at asking these questions, we will get some answers. Then what are we going to do with them?

Are there existing structures through which we can work? Do we need to support an intentional candidate for the school board? Is there a community group on social action? Asking the questions is the homework. It merely serves to *define* the task. Accomplishing it is going to mean, hard, long-haul work.

We Are Part of a Voting Precinct

Politics is an unavoidable involvement for the family who cares. There are only a few people whose *individual* acts will sway history. But history is regularly swayed by intentional groups.

This is an awesome fact. History *is* swayed. It behooves us to study through some current problems, that we may lend our weight lucidly and wisely to the task.

Wisely? Lucidly? How so?

The League of Women Voters can be one way. This is often a studying, researching, and vital group, and a pricker of community conscience. (It is a left-handed compliment that they have been referred to as the Plague of Little Women.) One woman was asked by her busy husband to join the League that she might become the "informed" member of the family in certain areas and pass on this information to the rest.

A stranger came to our town to speak to a university group. He had a Saturday free of appointments. So he spent it intentionally, poking around all over town, finding out what was here and what was not. He probably learned more that day about the educational facilities and recreational facilities, the churches, dives, slums, and suburbs, than most of the residents of this town will ever know. *We* could spend a Saturday—or several of them— like that.

Sister Margaret has a genuine concern for people caught in the lower income bracket. So she has armed herself with charts and documents, with pictures and slides (showing the rat holes, the exposed wiring, and the locked wash house). She has studied local housing requirements and building codes, is conversant with Federal laws, and has an honest awareness of how things really are. Thus equipped, she can serve as a thorn in the flesh to absentee landlords, to the housing administration, to promise-the-moon politicians, to semi-concerned church groups, and to city hall.

All this is part of the homework.

That done, we can proceed with the task. Knowing the needs, we can begin to formulate some structures.

Are there groups already working on the problem? Then that may be where we are needed. Or are there groups already set up who *could* meet these needs, if they had a spark plug?

We have ideal solutions in mind. These usually have to be tempered with reality.

"What we are called to do in this field and in every other is to choose the all-round best alternative (albeit a *mixed* good) and then give it our full support so that we give our weight to the advance—at least in a measure—of goodness in the world." [2]

[2] James Pike, *Doing the Truth* (New York: Macmillan, 1955), p. 111.

We can love people, and be sorry that they don't have things better. But it must be a love made valid through political structure and hard work, or it profiteth nothing.

We humankind are by nature parochial folk. But there is life beyond the county line. That life impinges upon our lives, and we cannot ignore it. The world has become a city. Transistor radios have made us one. More people have traveled farther, younger, oftener—have seen and heard and learned more about other parts of "this vehicle earth" than ever before. Many of our problems— the population explosion and air pollution among them—are worldwide in scope. A parochial point of view is no longer a valid or an honest one.

Our voting precinct is a place where we elect a county sheriff. But it is also the place where we vote for a president. Our voting box helps elect a man who will have a tremendous influence on the life of a nation and a world. We must choose the man who is *best* for the whole world; only so will he be best for this nation.

In recent elections, young people have been very active, often leading the rest of us, creating a new interest in national politics. They have added a new verve to politics. Many of these people were not old enough to vote, but were expressing an awareness that the world has outgrown provincialism.

It has. Twenty minutes of hydrogen warfare

49

could destroy the world. We'd *better* be world-conscious. Unchecked population increase affects us all. Pollution anywhere can make life less pleasant for all of us and may ultimately make the earth an unfit place to live.

Homework again. The man of faith should understand his world better than anyone else.

And questions again.

It took 18.5 million dollars to send up a Saturn rocket. It takes 3 million dollars an hour to wage war in Viet Nam. We decide.

If we could wage peace with the same dedication with which we wage war!

We decide.

We Are Part of a Church Congregation

Why?

Out of habit?

Do we go to church just to feel a little better, so we can face the week ahead?

Or because it is good for business?

Or for social prestige?

Or because that is where we see all our friends?

This really is not what the church was meant to be. This institution was meant to change history. Its task is to create the future of mankind. It's call is to enable men to realize their potential —to become fully human. I would like to be a part of that!

But to accomplish such a task, we will have to work at it. We, the church, must have a comprehensive mission that includes poverty and politics and dirty slum kids and pampered, sheltered suburbia. We must sing work songs as well as hymns—and sing both wholeheartedly.

But here is a structure in which intentional people can be trained to serve, and through which intentional people can mold the future.

How, then, do we begin?

By making the Sunday school class of which we are a part a real learning experience? By ordering contemporary literature, on our own if necessary, and hunting up a depth curriculum? By asking the right questions, at the right time? By speaking up when we have something worthy and honest to say? We may no longer have the option of avoiding a *teaching* responsibility.

How do we begin? By infiltrating the policy-making board? Or the finance committee? By joining the social concerns committee, and supporting those people who are consciously engaged in the task?

God *is* at work in the world today—in student unrest, in the laboratories of research scientists, in the striving of people to be free—and in the *seeking* church. Our task is to interpret God by collaborating with him.

Perhaps it is only when radical change cracks the hard shell of tradition that God can speak to us. We should be celebrating this now-we-can-hear-ness.

The same answers are not valid for everybody. For one family, intentional participation in society may mean moving to Malaysia. For another, it may be buying into a new apartment complex or renting an urban renewal unit. It may mean not moving at all, but staying where we are with the determination to be for *this* community what it needs.

We come to the church to worship, to be instructed in God's way, to be released into freedom, to be commissioned as a man-for-others. Here we train—here we receive inspiration both by the Word and by the support of the fellowship of the concerned.

But the task is to move out, into all of society—into all the channels through which God works in the world.

We gather to learn.

We scatter to witness, and to change the structure of society.

Chapter Four

The Family Celebrates

Here we are, a family—a unit bound together as in no other relationship.

Part of what makes us a unit is determined by law and custom. But most of what makes us a family is a matter of *esprit de corps*—a common understanding of our life together.

"The family needs help in maintaining a vivid identity. More fundamental than their doing things together is the need for finding a common goal and a way of saying who they are." [1]

Family celebrations (and we all have them) say who we are. They become meaningless if we have nothing to say about ourselves or about our mission. If, however, we undertake them intentionally, they can remind us of our past, and shove us into the future. They can call us to task on some occasions, and hold us up with the grace of our heritage on others.

Some rituals (celebrations) just happen. Some

[1] Roy W. Fairchild, "The Church Faces a Changing Family," *Social Progress Magazine.* (Issue on "The Church and Culture, Man"), 1957.

are deliberately initiated in order to express our family identity.

Holidays offer a ready-made opportunity for ritual. Perusal of the calendar shows many of both a religious and a cultural nature. A number of these are dates which need not command our attention—National Pickle Week, for instance. (Unless, of course, the intentional family *wants* to find out a thing or two about the growing and pickling of cucumbers.)

The intentional family will use opportunities, not superficially to "have a party," but to make themselves aware.

An exercise in intentional family living might be to set up a calendar—now—to help ourselves *prepare* for the celebration of days.

This could be done in family caucus. There will be special dates to record, birthdays and anniversaries, Easter, Thanksgiving and Christmas, Labor Day and the Fourth of July. We add others as we find them valid.

January got its name from Janus, a god of ancient Rome who had two faces. With such handy countenances he could look back to the past and forward to the future.

Perhaps mealtime on January 1 (whether or not it includes black-eyed peas) would give a family the opportunity to do just that—appraise the past and dedicate the future.

February 14 can be a sticky, sentimental mish-mash, or it can be an opportunity to express the loving concern in which each family member is held.

It is love which undergirds the mechanics of living. But love may need to be expressed to be remembered. And the expression sometimes comes hard. (The kid who has done some "durn fool thing"—and then cannot quite articulate "I'm sorry,"—picks up the trash in the yard, or keeps his room really clean for two whole days. The deed becomes his vehicle of expression.)

Valentine's Day offers a socially acceptable way for even the shyest to say, "I love you."

The forty days before Easter need not be just ordinary days. The traditional "sacrifice" for Lent, often meaningless, can be valid. My friend who gave up Cokes, and drank an uncola instead, was called to task because "you didn't really give up anything at all."

It was her attitude, though, that made it valid. She was not sacrificing to match or to pay for the suffering of Christ; but she was participating in a graphic reminder, calling her own self to remembrance by this small act. In doing so, she called me to remembrance, too, every time I saw her pass up a Coke.

Giving up something is not the only way of observing Lent. The *thoughtful* investment in a

CARE package, outgrowth of family awareness of world need, could be a worthy Lenten act.

One family tries to *give,* rather than give up. The first year their gift was to a child in the Headstart class for whom the eldest daughter was a volunteer worker. The child was bald—perfectly, completely bald—as a result of a serious illness. Daughter, in telling the family of her adventures on the job, mentioned the little girl who had no hair. And the family bought her a gift, intentionally—a simple and inexpensive wig. What they really gave the child was poise and gladness and self-esteem.

Lent can be taken as an opportunity for participating in full awareness in the drama of life. It prepares us for the celebration of Easter. Otherwise, Easter comes upon us too suddenly, like viewing the last act when we haven't seen the rest of the play.

It was Good Friday, and we went to the church for the evening service. The sanctuary was dim and gloomy.

Then Sunday morning came. Easter Sunday morning. Once again we stepped into the same sanctuary, only now it was brilliant with the dazzle of sun through stained glass, and with an altar banked high with white Easter lilies.

That simple, graphic contrast brought home to us what Easter really meant—light where there had been darkness; joy where there had been despair; and love, triumphant and deeply undergirding. It is a demanding, requiring love, for the dying and the living anew has to happen in us or it has not happened *for* us.

Somewhere, somehow, each family must find its own understanding of Easter, and its own way of celebrating the Christ event. It may be at a community sunrise service—or in watching the glory of the same sunrise from their own backyard. Whether the celebration is at the church altar or the family table, it is a time of remembering and of rejoicing.

The family will, of course, be very aware of the secular observance of Easter. The kindergartner will be coloring pictures of the Easter Bunny and warbling ditties about Peter Cottontail. Newspapers and T.V. will be full of come-on about new Easter outfits and hair styles and accessories. It is unrealistic for the family to try to ignore the customs of the culture that surrounds them. But it is quite possible to bring these customs into the Christian perspective through interpretation.

The festival of Easter is the oldest Christian observance on the church calendar. It is testimony to the great good news, brought to the despairing disciples, that the Christ who had taught them to live, and then who had himself been put to death, was alive, was risen! This testimony was joy indeed.

It is this joy that we celebrate. And it is this concept of new life which the child can appreciate, and through which he can come to terms with the secular custom.

According to one view, the name of the day, Easter, comes from Eostre—the name of an Anglo-Saxon goddess. But she was goddess of the dawn, and hence the word came to *mean* dawn—new life after night. (Our word *east* comes also from Eostre.) Even the rabbit fits in, as it was Eostre's symbol of new life.

We dye the eggs (traditionally, yellow for the returning sun, purple for the King of Life, and red for joy) in the good, warm-smelling, hint-of-vinegar kitchen, and we speak of them as symbols of new life. Just like the lilies that grow from dry brown bulbs—blooming triumphantly, to help us say what Easter means.

The first Easter happened during Passover week. Jesus was in Jerusalem to share in the celebration of that Jewish holy day. For a number of years thereafter, the dates of Passover determined the date for the observance of Easter. Passover did not always fall on Sunday, though, and some of the early Christians felt that the first Easter *had,* and that subsequent Easters *should.* So for a period of more than 200 years, Easter was celebrated on different dates in different places. Then in A.D. 325 the Council of Nicea set a date. Astronomers helped them establish it in relation to the spring moon.

A family can still anticipate the arrival of Easter by watching the moon. (March 21 is the first day of spring. Look for the first full moon after that date—and Easter is the next Sunday.)

There are ways of observing the customs of Easter that give them added meaning. The family that lingers around the supper table on a cold winter evening to plant a hyacinth bulb speaks of its blooming "in time for Easter"—and perhaps plants another one for an elderly neighbor to enjoy. And when it *does* bloom it is a beautiful and fragrant reminder of life triumphant.

The family of older children who color a few choice, old-country, "patterned-all-over" eggs for a special list of lonely friends may be saying something about loving concern.

The mother, making a new spring dress for a daughter who has outgrown the ones left from last year, can speak of the joyful custom of wearing new clothes for Easter which was kept by the early Christians—casting off that which is old, and putting on clean, new raiment, that we may step forward in newness of life.

The "Emmaus Walk" is an Easter stroll still popular in many countries on Easter Monday. European families and friends go for long walks in fields and forests, remembering.

Hot cross buns, served thoughtfully on Good

Friday, or on Easter morning, can become a meal of remembrance and of communion.

Easter is a time of joy. Its observance can be newly designed, or it can be woven through with the meaningfully used customs of the ages.

The British have a special and inimitable word for Mother's Day: they call it "Motheringtide"!

What *is* the role of Mother in the intentional family? Is she merely cook and housekeeper? (Oh yes, and chauffeur, laundress, secretary, nurse, et cetera ad infinitum.) Or should her role be something deeper—comforter, on occasion, or pricker of conscience? mediator and challenger? teacher and fellow learner?

In its observation of the day, the family says something about its opinion of the mother's role, whether it does so intentionally or otherwise.

It may be a time not only for the expression of love and appreciation for the mother, but also a time for the mother herself to evaluate her own responsibilities and to reinterpret her role. It is a changing role, and needs updating often.

A ritual for the occasion? Why not ask each member of the family to address a word to the mother, and then conclude with her thoughtful response. This is not a "Mother, I thank for for . . ." and a "You're welcome, my dear." It is, for each one, a serious taking up the responsibility for his role in the family, and an assuming of responsibility for one another.

Father's Day can become the same. Only more so. The role of the father is considerably more than that of wage earner. The intentional father is totally present to his family (which is more significant than just being there all the time). In a sense he must stand apart, watching all that goes on within his family—moving a too difficult obstacle for one child; leaving a challenging barrier for another; encouraging, denying, enabling, requiring, restraining. It was not casually that Jesus used the word "Father" in trying to explain the nature of God.

The father is head of the house and priest of the flock. Perhaps Father's Day is a good opportunity for him to make vocal his acceptance of that responsibility.

It is a good time, too, for each one to become aware of all the father must do just to keep the family going. Then, in expressing their appreciation, they offer him some of their own strength.

It is in such moments of trying to say who we are that we begin to *become* a family.

June 24 is Midsummer Night. In accordance with ancient custom (Druid, maybe?) this longest day of the year is the time for gathering the trash and burning it—symbolic of the burning of our past. That done, the intentional family moves out into the future. This is a sort of mid-year accounting, halfway between New Year's and New Year's.

Our national birthday happens in July—and we are not quite sure what to do with it.

There is a debt we owe, as a twentieth-century American family, to people whose dedication and suffering and high calling made it possible for us to live in a privileged nation. We in turn have the responsibility to make it what those patriots meant for it to be. As part of a family ritual for the Fourth of July, we would accept responsibility for our country, for its faults, its glories, its past, present, and future. Then, as world citizens, we would accept responsibility not only for our own country, but for the whole world.

Labor Day, the first Monday of September, is a good day for reminding ourselves of the worth and the privilege of work.

Our work is a task; let it be done with pride in the craftsmanship. The intentional family can call to mind the debt we owe to the men who collect the trash, who sweep the snow from the street, and who sell us groceries and gasoline. We owe a debt, too, to those who ponder the truths of the universe—those who teach, and stimulate us to ask and to think. The work of other men makes ours possible. It also calls to mind our obligation to work *for* other men.

The date varies, but the day is written across the minds of our children in capital letters: THE FIRST DAY OF SCHOOL.

Here are two rituals for its observance, both merely suggestions. Yours must be yours to be significant. Think through what *your* family needs to say to itself about school, and say it.

1.

Leader: We have made preparations for this day.

New jumpers have been completed.

New jeans have been purchased.

The smell of new crayons and the snap of a new notebook are part of our day.

But beyond this, and more important, is the real significance of the first day of school.

We stand on the threshold of adventure.

I charge you to seize this day, and learn! Contribute! Participate!

Parents: We send you out to be students.

Are you ready?

Children: (in spontaneous reply) Yes! We're ready.

2.

Father: We are deeply indebted to those who have gone before us, who

63

have accumulated knowledge and passed it on. We have benefitted from years and centuries of the research and mistakes and discoveries and enlightenment of these others.

Now it is our task to learn;

yours in a formal classroom, as students;

ours, as parents, learners also, and not exempt from growing in wisdom.

Unison Prayer: Thou, who art the beginning of wisdom and the source of all that is, we commit ourselves to the task of learning. We accept the heritage of the past. We accept the responsibility of learning from it, adding to it, and passing it on to the future. Amen.

Father: I send us out to be students, on behalf of all mankind. Amen.

Unison: Amen.

Rituals are not always religious, nor are they always serious. It is often those occasions of just plain fun that bring a family close together.

Not every family will celebrate Halloween in a special way—but it is a good opportunity for fun, in a "drought" time. It has been two months since picnics were possible, and it is still a while until snowmen can be made. So—in between, Halloween!

The mother who dressed up in black cape and hat to outspook the spooks with witchy laughter over the intercom, interjected an occasion of fun into family life. So did the father who dragged up a tub of water and brought out apples for bobbing.

We spend so much of our lives trying to make our children "be good" or "measure up" that sometimes we forget to have fun with them. A family is made up of the people we love the most; and they are the very ones with whom we should have the most fun. Starting now.

Then comes, by official decree, Thanksgiving.

We can stuff ourselves, or feed our souls. It is difficult to do both at once. We can celebrate our contingency by having malt-o-meal for dinner, but even this can become meaningless. Without an *expression* of what we are doing, and why, this would have no more significance than a forgetting-to-go-to-the-store change of menu.

(What would it do to your family if you really went through with this malt-o-meal bit—and then had just something simple like sandwiches for supper? Could it be used to call them to awareness of our undeserved blessings, and our inescapable responsibilities?)

One Thanksgiving dinner at Grandma's, just as

65

the turkey was ready to come out of the oven, the electricity went off—stove, lights, and all. And it was an evening meal. Grandpa stumped out to the barn and brought in an old coal-oil lamp, lit it, moved the sophisticated centerpiece, and plunked the lamp down in the middle of the table.

It became a ritual. Now that family *traditionally* eats, and gives thanks, by the light of a coal-oil lamp.

All of December becomes a ritual. Many of the traditional things we do, though, just happen. We do them because we have always done them.

The intentional family will *think through* its December rituals, using them to *say* what they mean about Christmas.

Perhaps a late-November family meeting can provide the setting in which the members can discuss together their December traditions. Some are sheer fun, and this makes them worthy. Some are others-centered, and are therefore valid. Some are outgrown, and should be cast aside. And some are missing. There are ways of expressing Christmas that we can appropriate. Or we can think through to some brand new ways of celebration that are unique to us alone. The intentional family sorts its customs, and saves, and savors, and prunes, thinking through and adding on.

Birthdays!

A child celebrates birthdays with the utter delight of being a year older. He relishes, embraces, each new year. It signifies a new status, a new maturity. Older now, he looks forward to new responsibilities and new privileges.

Birthdays should hold some of the same delight of anticipation for adults. We are older now, too, and should look forward to new horizons, new opportunities.

Each birthday reminds us, too, that we have one less year to live. This is an invitation not to morbid preoccupation, but rather to challenge. Whatever it is that we want to do with our lives, we'd best get on with it.

Life is like holding a magnifying glass in the sun. When it is focused just right, things begin to happen. Birthdays remind us to get our lives focused on what it is we intend to do. This accomplished, things begin to happen.

A ritual for a birthday should include an addressed word, which charges the individual with the importance of living responsibly.

A ritual should also call attention to the joy—the heady joy—of living.

"We charge you with taking up your new year intentionally, on behalf of all mankind.

"And we rejoice in, and celebrate, the years of your life!"

Something memorable happens when the daughter-bride and her parents find a moment of privacy just before the wedding ceremony in which to celebrate together their new roles. The daughter may address a word to her parents, thanking them for bringing her to this moment, and for releasing her to another relationship with their blessings. There may be a charge to worthiness by the parents. This special feeling of tenderness needs to be *said*. This is equally applicable to the groom and his family.

It is the *occasion* which makes the ritual necessary. It is the *ritual* which lends the occasion depth.

A new job is so very important in a family that it ought to be held up in ritual.

A father leaving home on a business trip can be sent out on behalf of the whole family.

The son whose band travels to the state capital to march in the inauguration parade is privileged to participate in an event which other members of his family will not be able to attend. If he is sent out by his family, as the official representative *of* the family, then in a sense they also participate.

Thus the very activities which tend to cause a family to grow apart bring them closer together.

The daughter going off to college, or the son into the service, particularly needs the addressed word of the family.

In any young person's life, the privilege of driving is a thrilling one. That it imposes upon him obligations and responsibilities of an awesome nature can be expressed in a ritual presentation of his own set of car keys. Not only would the parents charge the young driver with the life and the lives he now takes into his own hands, but the driver himself would be required to respond, in a sober and mature way.

Some calendars set apart other dates as significant. Rosh Hashanah, Yom Kippur, and Hanukkah, days of deep meaning to those of the Jewish faith, are certainly celebrations of which all should have some understanding. The Christian debt to the Jewish people is a great one. What better time to express this than on the occasion of Jewish holy days.

A family who has hosted a foreign student may find itself, years after, observing in its own way Ramadan or the Persian New Year. "How many miles to the heart of a friend?" Not too many, when thoughts are bound together by a common memory.

Sometimes by happy accident we learn of a custom from another land which speaks to our own family. We adopt it with enthusiasm, so that it becomes our custom, too. It was from a third-grade reader that we first learned of Boy's Day in Japan. What more delightful way of honoring our sons than by flying carp kites for them on the fifth day of the fifth month! Long a symbol of strength and perseverance, carp have a message for sons. (Sometimes inexpensive paper carp kites are available at an import shop. But just any old kite, flown together, makes May 5 an occasion.)

Its sister holiday, the third day of the third month, is Girl's Day in Japan. It is a time for lady-like dress-up tea parties, with the dolls as guests.

These days say something to the growing child about what it means to be a man and what it means to be a woman. But mostly they say that *the child is important.*

One year, after we had celebrated Mother's Day in May, and Father's Day in June, our sons inquired, "When is it Brother's Day?" "Why,—uh—in July!" And it was. We chose a particular day, packed a picnic lunch, and went to the zoo. How many miles to the heart of a child? Not so many, when thoughts are bound together by a common memory.

The giving of thanks before a meal reminds us that every day is a holy day, a gift-of-God day. The saying of grace can be as mechanical as a thoughtless bedtime "Now I lay me down to sleep . . ." or as spontaneous and cup-overflowing as a sudden *need* to sing the doxology.

Herein lies a paradox: it takes an awareness of the holy nature of an ordinary day to keep the grace from being mechanical; but sometimes it is the automatic pause for grace that reminds us of this holy day.

The five-year-old's thanks for French fried potatoes and ketchup, by name, is a valid and meaningful grace. So, too, is the majestic tone of a centuries-old prayer of the early church. Life has many moods, and the psalm of thanksgiving may be sung to many tunes.

Contemporary ones, too, by the way. As meaningful as *Old 100th* is on some occasions, the words take on a new enthusiasm (an *en-theos,* a with-Godness) when sung to the tune of *Jamaica Farewell.* Or to some other tune of your own choosing. Experimenting with new ways of doing things is not "tampering with that which is holy." It may be a way of making it more holy.

The very breaking of bread was once made holy, and the sharing of food is a sacrament. The purpose of each meal is something more than the nourishment of the body. Something had to die, that I might live. An animal gave its life, a plant gave its life, men gave their labor. Backs ache that I might eat a potato. So a ritual of grace before a meal should be both a time of thanks to God for life itself, and a time of remembrance of what life costs.

How to say it? That depends upon the day, and the moment, and the mood. But the family that can learn to express its thanks simply, and

71

honestly, and often spontaneously, may be expressing it best.

Here are a few rituals of grace that may fit into certain moments around the altar of the dining table.

(May be sung. Use the hymn tune, "Lord, Speak to Me." Canonbury LM 88.88)

> We thank Thee, Lord, for daily bread,
> For by Thy love our souls are fed.
> Help us to grow more like to Thee
> This day and through eternity.

Our heavenly Father, we thank thee that—
  Back of the loaf is the snowy flour,
  And back of the flour the mill,
  And back of the mill is the wheat and the shower,
  And the sun and the Father's will. Amen.

Old Scottish Grace:

Some ha' meat and canna eat, and some ha' none
  that want it,
But we ha' meat, and we can eat, and so the Lord
  be thanket.

> If we have earned the right to eat this bread,
> Happy indeed are we,
> But if unmerited Thy gifts to us,
> May we more thankful be.

There are occasions when a member of the family *seeks out* a ritual to give himself the strength he may need. We were privileged to see this happen when Melissa, who is eight, remarked one afternoon, "Did Martha sing for the PTA when she was in the second grade?"

"Oh, I guess she might have. Are you going to sing for PTA?"

"Yes," said Melissa, smiling graciously. "Tomorrow night."

Oh, no! *Any* other night would have been fine. But that one was already committed. Invited to a banquet by friends, two weeks in advance, we had checked the calendar, found the date quite clear, and accepted with pleasure. Tickets were already bought. We simply could not go to hear Melissa's class sing.

I explained to Melissa, as gently as I could. She was keenly disappointed, but took it rather nobly. With sudden inspiration, I asked what time tomorrow her class would be *practicing* for the program: I could go listen to them practice. She told me, and the crisis was over . . .

. . . until Melissa came in from school the next afternoon. "Mother," she said, calling me to account. "You didn't come to hear us sing." I had forgotten. Trapped in my own concentration on another project, I had forgotten. How I wished for a hole to crawl in, or some real sackcloth and ashes to demonstrate for her my sorrow and chagrin.

This second disappointment was too much, and the tears came uncontrollably. She cried most of the afternoon. Then she summoned her resources and prepared to face life anyway.

Melissa had received, just a few days before, a small round box of cheeses, each one a little foil-wrapped wedge fitting into the wagon wheel. It was a special gift, one she had coveted for a long while. Melissa went to the refrigerator and selected a wedge of cheese. Then she peeled it, very carefully. She found a little bottle of ancient candy beads, remnant of some long-forgotten birthday cake. Pouring these in a pan, she carefully set the cheese down on them, on each of its sides, studding it with the bright, hard bits. Then she set the cheese on top of a little plastic box, and set two tiny candles in it, just so.

"Mother," she addressed me solemnly, "could we all come together for a minute?" I was aware of the importance of the moment, and called the family in from the basketball game and the funnies and the shower. We stood around the kitchen table, while Melissa addressed a word. With the solemnity that only a very small eight-year-old can muster, she began:

"Tonight we celebrate two very important things. One is that Mother and Daddy are going to a banquet, and that is very important to them. The other is that I am going to sing for the PTA, and that is very important to me. One of these candles is for the banquet, and one is for the singing. I would like for my Mother and Daddy to light them." She handed us the matches, and we lit the candles.

"Now," she turned to her brothers, "Jim and Mark, you may blow the candles out." (Even big brothers, on such occasions, do not snicker.)

"Martha," she turned to her sister, "you may remove the candles." Then Melissa very carefully sliced the little wedge of cheese into six bites. We all prepared ourselves, for we had tasted the cheese before and found it awful, and the candy bits did not help it any. Martha, who really just can't go cheese anyway, was relieved when Melissa dropped one minuscule serving on the floor, and then said that could be Martha's. The rest of us received our graciously offered servings and ate them, and were dismissed.

Melissa had constructed a ritual to say to herself, "I can cope," and to say to us, "I really do understand, and it is all right." I shall not soon forget. She celebrated life as it was—even as she was painfully aware that in *that* circumstance it was not beautiful and good.

(By way of postscript, Melissa had two brothers, one sister, and a "big girl" friend to accompany her to PTA—and a loving neighbor to tell her afterward how nice it sounded.)

Chapter Five

The Family Demonstrates

It's an old Greek word—*graphics* (or *graphikos*) —and it means "the expression of ideas by means of lines, marks, or characters impressed on a surface."

Precisely. That's what makes it valid. We cannot *draw* vagaries and ambiguities. The human mind, thrown out of gear, can idle along with fuzzy thinking. But once we get out a pencil and try to *draw it out* or *write it down,* we must grapple with specifics. It is at this point that graphics become a tool for the intentional family.

Graphics serve another purpose: they wrap a lot of meaning in a little package.

 says much more than "a horizontal line intersecting a vertical line."

speaks of a long tradition of courage and dedication and martyrdom. The two curves depict far more than the crude illustration of a fish.

How does this fit in with family living? Can pictures and drawings help us say who we are and what we are about? Emphatically!

F'rinstance:

One family made a crest. They *decided,* as a family, what they really wanted to say about themselves—and then they incorporated it into a design, painted it onto a shield-shaped board, and hung it on the wall. The family circle is the basic

shape. The Christian Chi-Rho is used as a symbol of faith, together with the lamp of learning. The globe speaks of membership in a world community, and the sarape signifies residence in the Southwest. The yin-yang symbol in the lower right is from the Orient, and expresses the duality of life and of the universe: good-bad, happy-sad, life-death, man-woman, parent-child, old-young—each flowing into the other, inseparable and mutually contributive. A rural past and an urban present are depicted. And of course the family name is declared.

Another family used maps of Norway and Texas to represent its heritage, and has other symbols of vocation and dream. No two crests will be alike, because no two families are alike.

One family built a cornice over the dining table window, both to say something about their faith and to call themselves to remembrance.

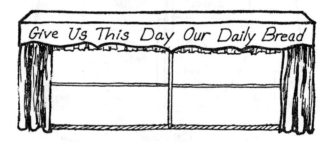

Seeing the cornice, and finding that it spoke also to them, another family adapted the message to its own past.

They find in its Shona words "Our Father, Who Art in Heaven") a reminder of an African past and of a present commitment. It becomes also a way of saying to those who come in, "This we believe."

Sometimes a surname offers the opportunity to say something.

It's just a sign out front, but it says, "A *family* lives here. And every member of it is important and has his own distinctive place."

A family whose vocation deals with the church

 on the university campus worked out a symbol combining the lamp of learning with the early Christian pictograph of the fish.

A specific symbol is not the only way in which we say to the world who we are, or what we believe, or where our interests lie. These things are expressed in all kinds of ways.

The decor of a home speaks volumes to the guest who enters. It can be attractive and inviting without being so rigidly French provincial that there is no place to put a prized trophy or a second-grader's drawing. A too-strict regard for the rules of interior design may rob a home of the spontaneity that makes it unique and expressive.

Why *not* put the fistful of alley-weed flowers in a conspicuous place in the living room? If they are a gift of love, they *deserve* a place of honor. Why *not* put up the wooden mask, memento of the family's trip to Mexico, even in the midst of the early American decor? Must Grandma be denied her favorite rocker or Dad his easy chair because they destroy the Mediterranean mood of the living room suite? The bright colors of Martha's mosaic parrot may not match anything else in the room, but they cheer me every time I walk by. They bring to mind, as no store-bought accessory could, the gift that Martha is.

The intentional family may hang a picture on the wall, and use it to address a word. Any one of a number of pictures, if thoughtfully and carefully selected, may hold within it a real significance. Larsen's "Head of Christ," or Picasso's "Guernica," either one, can be meaningless. Or either one can be worthy and singularly meaningful, if intentionally used.

And the acquisition of a picture need not strain the family budget. One cut from a magazine and mounted on fiber board can come through loud and clear. Sometimes good copies can be checked out from the public library.

Graphics are only a tool. Decor does not *make* a room. Sometimes a companionable warmth is achieved when the furnishings are merely Early Attic. Sometimes that same inviting hospitality can permeate a Spanish or Danish modern interior design.

An overdose of gadgets can be depressing. Too many gewgaws on the coffee table, too many things hanging on the wall, are still clutter, no matter how beautiful each piece may be. A museum is an interesting place to visit, but a frustrating place in which to live. Why not *alternate* what is out on the coffee table, enjoying each item in turn by according it a place of honor all its own?

My friend wailed, "What I really need is more cabinet space." Her more efficient neighbor countered: "No. What you really need is this much cabinet space, maybe less—and a whole lot less junk. You cannot operate effectively with so many *things*. Decide what you really need in order to get the task done, and then get rid of the rest."

We have a word for it—"impedimenta." We got it from the conquering army of the old Roman

Empire, which tagged its accumulation of personal baggage "Impedimenta." And they considered it a real impediment, a distinct encumberance. They much preferred to travel light.

It is still true. When we are too heavily burdened with *things,* we are not really free to travel— whatever kind of traveling we have in mind. There is a very real sense of lightness and freedom that happens when we clean out the hall closet and throw away all the junk!

It is not necessary for any one of us to do or buy or plant or keep that which the Joneses have. My neighbor has a green thumb. For her, flowers are a challenge and a comfort and a gift of God. What she does with them is a gift to the whole community. So for her, time spent in the yard is time well spent.

But my thumb—*thumbs,* all ten of them—can't make things grow. For me to try to make my yard look like hers would be both a dishonesty and an extremely heavy burden. So why don't I *intentionally* plant shrubs instead of flowers? She can bring me a bouquet of flowers, and I shall take her a loaf of freshly baked bread, and we shall both be doubly blessed.

Thus both exterior and interior decor become graphic. They need not proclaim that landscaping and interior design are among my engrossing interests, if they are not. Graphics are only a tool, and not an end in themselves.

A TOOL IS TO USE

For the intentional family, a "tool" can be used
deliberately. A bulletin board, for instance. It may
be a nicely framed cork type—or a scrap of left-
over Celotex, or a monstrous four-by-eight sheet
of fiberboard bought for the purpose.

And it ought to be placed in a spot handy for
looking. (By the breakfast table? Where else
would we all have time really to look at what's
on it?)

A bulletin board is a place to post schedules—
but it can be much more. It can provide a place
for saying more important things, some of which
are difficult to articulate.

These items, among many others, have appeared
at different times on family bulletin boards:

Norman Rockwell's magazine-cover painting of
people of many faiths, with its cryptic message,
"Do unto others . . ."

A display of madonna pictures, including one by
Raphael, one of an Indian mother and child,
one of a little girl and her doll, one from Africa,
another from Hungary.

A Spanish vocabulary list.

A map of somewhere, that one of the kids was
asking a question about yesterday.

A center-fold magazine picture of a van unloading the goods of a just-moving-in family. In front of the truck, confronting each other, stand the "new" kids, who are black, facing the "old" kids, who are white. But the Negro boy is holding a baseball glove behind him, and one of the white boys is leaning on a bat.

An article on safe driving, torn from a magazine, posted without comment. The teen-ager for whose benefit it was clipped read it with interest—and might well have resented Mama handing it to him with a "Here. Read this."

A poster (also clipped from a magazine) with a brief message in contemporary lettering:

> To Do a Common Thing
> Uncommonly Well . . .

And another adage:

> Pray devoutly;
> hammer stoutly.

A copy of *Desiderata* ("Go placidly amid the noise and haste . . .")

A first-grader's self-portrait, and a second-grader's forthright attempt at a family portrait.

News clippings of a high school trip which will involve one of the kids.

And lists.

And schedules.

And a calendar.

A clipping on the chemical production of an enzyme. Calling it to attention thus enables the family to say, "See, here is God at work in the world today."

Side by side, a copy of Van Gogh's "Starry Night" and a picture in color of the earth as the astronauts saw it from their moon orbit.

Avoiding the clutter of too-many-things-at-once, we can use the family bulletin board to announce, point out, teach, stimulate, and, on occasion, to address a word.

One last graphic deserves mention—the making of a collage. Save an evening, and lots of old magazines. Scrounge some scissors and paste. Some of the family won't know what gives, so a word of explanation would be in order. "Just cut out and paste (on a sheet of construction paper, or half a file folder, or a grocery sack) pictures or words that will go together to express "This is the Real Me," or "This is my view of the world."

One father made a collage on his view of the world in which he portrayed solid chaos in black and white, clipping pictures of riots and war and car wrecks and rubble. Then superimposed on such a background was the simple vivid bright-color word (cut from a soap ad) JOY!

Making a collage might become an opportunity through which each of us can see another, but also through which we can see ourselves. It may give one a chance to say in a new way something for which he cannot find words. (A child will sometimes express fears through this art form that he cannot bring himself to admit in words—and in the expression find release.)

Well, a graphic is only a tool. But it may, on occasion, be a useful one, helping the intentional family express who it is and what it is about.

Chapter Six

The Required Adventure

Three astronauts, orbiting the moon, looked back through 228,000 miles of space at little Earth. They could bring whole continents, even an entire hemisphere, within their range of vision. And they spoke of the rest of us, all riding together on this earth-ball.

All riding together. Like the quaint old-fashioned family in a touring car—only updated, and multimagnified—the family of man is all riding together on the vehicle Earth.

The intentional family has an imperative to learn all it can about these others with whom we ride.

And "learn" is a verb of the present tense. Webster says that it is "to gain knowledge or understanding by study and investigation." This is something more, then, than the casual acquisition of a few facts. It is deliberate and planned.

Oh, we *learn* a certain number of things almost without effort. The blurb on the back of the cereal box tells us Willy Mays's batting average and the importance of the B vitamins. Those two- and three-line newspaper fillers inform us that Chile is exporting tin this year, and that rainfall has been a record low in Jubbulpore. The front page of the newspaper has a number of things to say about a war in Viet Nam. It does not tell us, however, what the people are like, what their history and customs and culture have been, or what their future holds.

What we learn casually just isn't enough. Random facts are really nothing more than random facts—until we grasp them, and examine them, and go further into them, and study, using them as starting points for deliberate investigation.

Real learning, then, requires a curriculum, a *plan* for family study. It will be as individual as a budget, tailored to the particular interests of a family. But it must be an *intentional* plan, or it will never happen.

So what are we going to study? "All Mankind" is a vague oblong abstraction. But we can narrow it down to a particular culture—for a specific length of time—and we have something on which to work.

A family might begin with a month's investigation of the African culture. And they might decide that their course of study will take place at suppertime, for the simple and practical reason that it seems to be the only time when everyone is present. Besides, an informal situation around the table is more fun and less inhibiting than sitting

THE REQUIRED ADVENTURE

stiffly on the couch, or in chairs lined up like a classroom.

Once we get into the swing of an Africa study, all manner of things may fit in. Becky remembers a singing grace she learned at vacation church school last summer. Mark hunts up the National Geographic series on the Kariba Gorge—and discovers that quite likely the whole history of mankind began there. Newspaper articles on Africa that went unnoticed before suddenly leap out as though set in bigger, blacker type. Newly aware, the family begins to see and hear and notice as never before.

To give context to all this, various members of the family do some background study, digging up facts to share. Perhaps a senior makes a free-form map for the bulletin board on which the others can record places of note—Cape Town, Durban, the gold and diamond mines near Johannesburg, new nations, old deserts . . .

But this is no dull, prosaic class-at-the-supper-table! There are *fun* things to learn! A volume or two of UNICEF's *Hi, Neighbor* will tell how they play hopscotch in one part of Africa—how they say thank you, or make candy, or run relays in another. A record or two (including some from the "Top Twenty" most of the time) will be good examples of the contribution of African "beat" to American music.

THE INTENTIONAL FAMILY

There are things to strive for, as the family studies:

> a sense of the *humanity* of the culture . . .
> a sense of history, and of current politics . . .
> an appreciation of the religion . . .
> an awareness of contribution . . .
> all seasoned, perhaps, with art and music and dance.

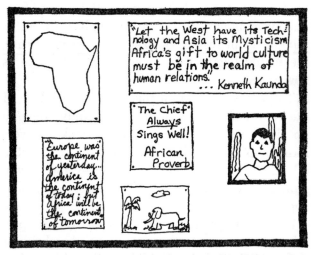

Now, what used to be an ordinary Monday night supper finds the family sitting down to a meal that includes pineapple and bananas and bomba (a Congolese chicken stew with peanuts in it) with cola to drink, since that came to us from Nigeria—while they listen to "the beat" on stereo, and look at the map and pictures and quotations on the bulletin board, and talk and share and learn about what Tom Mboya called *"The* continent of tomorrow." It may be that the intentional meal is scheduled only on Mondays, but somehow it laps over into the conversations of other meals on other nights, and a family is made aware. It laps over, too, into classes at school, and discussions with friends—into the casual reading of a newspaper, and we are made aware.

This could be a springboard for the systematic *study* of the cultures of the world. It will not be an attempt to learn everything there is to know about any one of them—but it will be an effort to sharpen our senses and our sensitivities.

The choice of what culture to study may be triggered by the world situation. Viet Nam? The Black Revolution in America? Indonesia? It may be triggered by a chance magazine article—or by Craig's library book, or Linda's social studies topic, or Ed's stamp collection. And it may be the outgrowth of a friendship with a foreign student, or of the correspondence with a pen pal.

Cultural studies are not the only curriculum

options. Certain times of year lend themselves to an extended (and *intentional*) study of nature. This may involve field trips; night sessions to study the stars; activities, such as the making of a mushroom spore print, or an ant farm, or a blueprint of a leaf; or the capturing on paper of the delicate architecture of a spider's web. (What a nice time to be reading *Charlotte's Web* as a bedtime story!)

Nature study may involve a safari in our own backyard. Thoreau, you remember, "traveled widely in Concord." Armed with a magnifying glass and a sharpened curiosity, we stalk down strange creatures like a daddy longlegs, who has his eyes on a sort of "conning tower" in the middle of his back; and a June bug, whose magnified face looks like that of an amiable puppy, with antennae like a pair of palm leaf fans waving ridiculously where the ears should be. We'll find sharp-beaked aphids attacking plants, and fierce meat-eating lady bugs attacking aphids—and perhaps a strange praying mantis, whose pious pose is merely in anticipation of reaching out to grab something for lunch, even if it happens to be his own kith and kin! Talk about drama!

A nature study could also be a study on ecology, topic of the world's sudden concern with pollution. One likely result of such a study would be a new awareness on the part of the family of their own contribution to the problem.

A time schedule, like the choice of topic, must be individually tailored. A one-meal-a-week study may require three month's duration to reach a worthwhile depth. An every-morning-at-breakfast pursuit might involve a monthly change of topic.

One family set up a course of study around these interrelated and progressive topics:

1. The Individual and Society	2. Black Man (African Culture)	3. Society (What makes it tick?)	4. Yellow Man (Oriental Culture)
5 This Community	6. Red Man in Latin America	7. The Nation	8. White Man (Western Culture)
9. The World	10. Brown Man (India)	11. Natural Science	12. Tan Man (Middle East)

Another family might undertake a study of world religions: Animism, Buddhism, Confucianism, Hinduism, Islam, Judaism, Zoroastrianism, and Christianity.

Whatever the topic, it's a family affair. If we are going to study Japan, and *I* tell 'em all about it—"blah, blah, blah"—that can get pretty sticky. But if second-grader Melissa shows a Japanese art form, and tells us in her own way how it differs from Western art—well, we're going to listen! The variety of the contributions of the kindergartner and Dad and Buddy and Grandma does indeed add spice to the study. Each has a real obligation to participate, and a real obligation to listen to and honor the contributions of the others.

There will be—should be—"extracurricular" learning within the intentional family. The course of study at home may be Africa right now. But if Suzie learns some perfectly delightful new thing at school about New Zealand—or Nevada—it needs to be shared. And the sharing needs to be honored.

Conversation goes well with a meal, and it need not deteriorate into a gripe session or a gossip session. Remember the Galbraiths in *Cheaper By the Dozen?* Intentional table talk was part of their way of life. The Joseph Kennedy family, the Rockefellers, and numbers of others, have deliberately guided the conversation at a meal into channels that would be instructive and constructive, and of benefit to a growing family. What better way—or time—for stretching the mind!

All this ought to be *fun*, whether it is the depth study or the casual looking-up-to-find-the-answer to "What's a runcible spoon?" There is a *delight* in learning something new.

There is also, lest we forget, an imperative to learn. To live dangerously in these days is unavoidable, but to live ignorantly is inexcusable.

The intentional family has an imperative also to contribute. And this we cannot do, ignorantly. Down through history, the people who have contributed the most have been the ones who *knew* the most, and who then used what they knew for the good of all mankind.

Chapter Seven

Management

The only way in which I can adequately love my family is by setting up a structure that will enable us to conduct our living effectively.

A family council can be such a tool.

The options in the operation of a family are three: democracy, dictatorship, or anarchy. We decide.

We are afraid of democracy.

Very few of us really want a dictatorship.

And so, by default, we drift into anarchy.

Sometimes, when the anarchy becomes more than we can stand, we alternate between brief periods of tyranny and returns to anarchy. This merely serves to muddy the waters still more, and breeds further insecurity for everybody concerned.

A reasonable approach to conducting the family's life is through a family council. This is no formidable chore. Nor does it mean that the parents abdicate and let the kids take over and run the establishment, just because they happen to be in the majority.

It is simply a calling together of the family group to make some plans, to set up some prerogatives, and to iron out some problems.

No time for a family council? It can *save* considerably more time than it requires. Eliminating a lot of fuss, and nit-picking, a lot of piddling and aimlessness, it *creates* time.

Can't figure out when on earth your family could possibly all get together for a weekly meeting? If it were important enough for a family to have this meeting, it might have to be scheduled instead of something else. Set a time. Having done so, reserve it for this purpose. Let it be a requirement that everyone be present. Other activities need not encroach on this one.

We decide to have time, or we decide *not* to have time.

What happens at a family council meeting?
Here is one approach:

Opening Ritual:

The members of this household and of the Family of God call themselves to attention. (Or use whatever terms you choose to state that this is indeed an intentional meeting, and that it is held up in the light of the very best that we know.)

Happenings of the Week
    a. In the world   (This informal time for
    b. In this nation   remembering what is go-
    c. and state   ing on around us reminds
    d. and community   us that we are apart of

e. and in this family the whole world, and that the happenings everywhere are an influence on our lives.)

Celebrations
A birthday? anniversary? special occasion?

(Here is an opportunity to dramatize these events for this family, and in doing so to set them in memory.)

Plans for next week
Individual (each member of the family replying) Family

(The mutual concern of the family for its members lays a claim on each individual as they mutually expedite joint and separate activities.)

A part of this planning may include talking through some problems, recognizing friction, and perhaps arriving at a family decision. Is one child monopolizing the phone? Does one, because he talks loudest, get more than his share of privileges? Is one making a pest of himself? How are things going? Does one child have a real *need* for a pair of tennis shoes, and ask that they be figured into the budget?

Accountability (This provides occasion for the family to call each of its mem-

	bers to a moment of self-recognition, lovingly, objectively, and in acceptance.)
Absolution	(Remember? We are accepted. We are given permission to be ourselves.)
Benediction	The world is yours, to live in and to change. Amen.

Not every decision should be made in family council. Nor is this a place for the one-for-one voting of a pure democracy. Actually, this is not the place for *voting* at all. Decisions should be reached by consensus rather than poll. (There is real psychological basis for this: if one votes, he feels a defensive obligation to uphold his original opinion. But if the decision was reached through open discussion and perhaps mutual compromise, there is no need to be defensive.)

It is not practical for children to be called upon to make decisions for which they are neither responsible nor prepared. Small children would not be capable of helping make a decision whether a father's change of jobs would be a wise move. But the small children need to be considered. And they need to have this and other family matters talked over with them, as concerned members of the family.

Mrs. Dale was faced with a dilemma after the

death of her husband. She could get a job and thus afford to keep up payments on the big house. Or they could move to a smaller house in another neighborhood, and she could continue to be at home with and for the children. She felt the decision was not hers to make. So she called her three children, ages twelve to sixteen, together to discuss it. The matter concerned them all.

The family-in-conference helps children learn how decisions are reached. And when children are *really* listened to, as persons of worth, they make some very valid suggestions.

Which decision can children legitimately help make? Each family works out its own format. If the family conference is a plan initiated when the children are small, they grow up participating. The whole family becomes more practiced in the processes of creative discussion. The adults find themselves making more responsible decisions because of the deliberate examination of alternatives. It is more difficult to *begin* to have family conferences after the children are older—to *decide* what to decide. But it is worth the effort, worth the awkwardness of beginning, worth the becoming-vulnerable-before-one-another, to start. The family council gives a structure through which we can state our purpose, remind ourselves of what we are about, and implement the necessary deed.

Time Management

The intentional family establishes early some prerogatives as to how it intends to use its daily allotment of twenty-four hours. If there are no goals, there is really very little point in managing time. If goals are real and clear, there is an imperative to spend wisely the time we have.

Using time wisely does not mean just the unswerving tenacity of plowing doggedly toward a destination, hating every minute of it. Rest, recreation, and renewal are also important.

What the intentional family is trying to avoid is *wasting* time. It is quite all right, for instance, to lie down for a thirty-minute afternoon nap when you really need the rest. But it is perfectly exhausting to lie in bed for half an hour, thinking all the while, "I really *should* be . . ."

We manage to waste time in such useless ways. Trying to decide where to begin, for instance. Backtracking. Wild goose-chasing. Woolgathering. Soap-opera or sports-event–watching to the point of excess. And pure unadulterated inefficiency. Some things are of questionable value *per se;* others become thefts of time because of the too-muchness. Bowling, which in itself is a wholesome sport, can become an insidious thing, robbing a family of its parents.

There are ways in which an intentional family can *add* to its supply of time. One is the simple expedient of getting up a little earlier every morning. We all need a certain amount of sleep. Most of us probably do not need as much as we allow ourselves, however, and could get along just as well with less. It is amazing what an additional thirty minutes in the morning can make possible.

The accepted practice for establishing the family's rising time seems to be: deciding upon the absolute latest moment that will still allow us to get where we need to be by the time we *have* to be there. Rush! Dither! Frustration! This leaves no margin for finding clean socks or the homework paper she knows she put *somewhere,* or for the discovery that someone finished off the last of the milk before bedtime last night.

Getting up thirty minutes earlier gets the family off on its way calmly and collectedly. If the boys have made their beds and cleared off the desk, they have probably come across the report or book that was to be taken to school. Less is forgotten, fewer naggings are hurled, tempers are more even. Each member of the family leaves home primed for the day. There will be other crises to face later on; how much better to have had a clean start.

Getting up earlier still may enable parents to have a quiet time of their own. It may be a time of prayer, of quiet exultation, and of dedication of the day. It is even a good time for study.

There are other ways of adding time. Organizing what we do is one of these. A grocery list is a case in point. We run to the store to get some milk. Later on we realize that we really don't have anything for supper, so we go back to the store. And then, *after* we get back home, we remember the suit that must be picked up at the cleaners. A plan, to accomplish all these in one trip while Martha is having her music lesson, would be a real time-saver. (Gas-saver, too.) Routing the accumulated errands is a significant saving. Mostly, this is just a matter of thinking ahead, and working with a plan, intentionally.

Menu-planning is another practical approach. The mother who plans ahead can make intelligent decisions on what the family will require. She generally ends up with better-balanced and more varied meals which cost less and take less time to prepare. These are the assets of management.

Schedules of all sorts create time. They eliminate the waste of indecisiveness, for they are "pre-thought." When schedules become inflexible, however, we abdicate our will to a piece of paper and become enslaved. A person too entrenched in a schedule is no longer *available* to the family. But the effective accomplishment of the chores because of a schedule enables us to have time for a picnic, or time to watch with a child the fascinating progress of an inchworm crossing the windowsill.

Added time happens when we *wait* intentionally. Everyone has some waiting to do. It may be in the doctor's office, or at the commuter-train station, or for the kids after each of their involvements. Having an intentionally chosen book in the car—or in purse or pocket—can make even waiting a time well spent. One intentional public figure buys paperback books almost exclusively. When he finishes one, if it is not something he wishes to keep, he leaves it—on the plane, in the lobby—for someone else to read. If he finds in it something he really wants to save, he simply tears it out and throws the rest of the book away. The book was sufficiently inexpensive that he can afford to do this, and he has what he wants without the impedimenta of the other 235 pages.

Not only books but notebooks are good timesavers. There are many choice things that we see or hear. And if we do not have something at hand on which to write them down, they get away. Here, too, is a good place to do some planning for the rest of the week, or to start a letter.

Involved in a car pool? *Use* the time it takes going to school or work every day. A group of men with a twenty-minute twice-a-day trip together on the freeway can get into some deep and illuminating discussions, if some among them are willing to give it a try. Or they can take turns doing some worthy reading. Or talking through some community problems.

If the car pool is of the juvenile variety, a mother who sings can make a real contribution by teaching some fun songs to the gang en route to school. And if, on Tuesday, it's the monotone mother who drives, she can from time to time interject the provocative question into the general chatter, and become a real teacher of philosophy. Wednesday's driver might throw in an occasional observation on nature in the ever-changing world outside the car. And Thursday's chauffeur may contribute a thought or two on current issues. All this becomes the *bonus* of an intentional car pool, and everyone's day is enriched.

Adding time happens when we seize that "just thirty minutes before it is time to . . ." Those half-hours get away, simply frittered. But in an intentionaly seized half-hour, you can put in a hem. Or clean the furnace filter. Or prune one rose bush. Or clean out a drawer. Or fix a doorknob, or repair a little red wagon. Making deliberate use of these small segments of time accomplishes all manner of wonders.

One thing more. One small, important thing more. *Putting things away* is an almost unparalleled saver of time. (How long have you looked for the tweezers, knowing they were supposed to be in the little box on the dresser? If only someone had put them away, you would have saved seventeen minutes and ten millimeters of blood pressure. And that would have given you the time required to hunt the screwdriver that you yourself forgot to put away.)

Consistent straightening up and putting away saves time. Lots of time.

How are we going to spend all this time that has been saved? Efficiency expert John Galbraith would have retorted, "Playing mumblety-peg, if that's what you *want* to do!"

Time for fun *should* be part of family living. *And it should be jealously preserved.* The attitude of levity is extremely important to the psychological health of the family.

Fun has many facets. Some families go camping. Some families play tennis. Some build stereo sets, or keep bees, or watch stars, or hunt rocks, or hike in the woods. These are worthy pursuits, and part of the growth of people.

But fun is in little ways, too.

Did you know that one penny piece of bubble gum, having been sufficiently masticated, can be stretched a full city block? (Mike has verified this fact with research and experiment.)

Fun is the permission of the attitude of levity. It happens only when people are relaxed. The person who is trying too hard to be intentional can move in a fog of serious contemplation that dampens the spirits of those around him. Walking around under a cloud of black worry and borrowed trouble like Joe Bftsplk merely increases the problems. It contributes nothing to their solution, and at the same time robs us of today. Better to do our homework; better to set aside a think-time. Then in uninterrupted concentration we can take out the problems, look them square in the face, decide what possible solutions are available, and make the necessary moves.

Having done that, we are free to enjoy *this* moment—free to see and enjoy our children, to listen to their laughter, and to add to it some of our own.

It was an informal sort of company, sitting around the table having lunch. "This is dessert," said the mother, handing over a sack of large scalloped ginger snaps. Gene took one, considered it thoughtfully, and said, "I'll bet I can eat the scallops off the edges before you can!" Everyone present took up the challenge, and the race was on. Because of the fun, it was a memorable moment.

Sometimes fun happens accidentally, and we have only to recognize and enjoy it. Sometimes it can be deliberately interjected into the family's day. *Save* the good joke; bring in the delicate seedpod of a milkweed. Make a Snoopy-shaped birthday cake, or a chemical garden. Decorate for an occasion; celebrate Tuesday! Isn't home fun to come home to?

The investment of time is frequently mentioned

in considering the family's use of television. When is TV worth it? There are some excellent natural science specials on from time to time. There are some outstanding plays, some splendid portrayals of people who are part of our past. Socrates will always be more real to those who saw "Barefoot in Athens," and Mark Twain and Oliver Wendell Holmes to those who saw them portrayed on television.

And did you ever try *theologizing* a Charlie Brown special? (Read *The Gospel According to Peanuts* for some real meaning behind the sayings and doings of Charlie-All-of-Us-Brown.)

Is there an educational TV channel in your area? Do you ever turn it on? It can be most interesting as well as instructive.

Of course, all this means the family must look ahead on a T.V. schedule and plan other events around the worthy programs. It means intentionally remembering that we gather on Tuesday night at 7:00 this week for the worthwhile investment of a segment of time.

There are times, too, when the TV should be intentionally turned off.

Some families intentionally do not have television at all, in order to have more time for reading aloud and for conversation.

Either way, there is no need to become enslaved by a square box of tubes and transistors and enigmatic circuits.

Time is for savoring.

She will never be two again. We will never have another fifth (or twenty-fifth) anniversary.

Savor these irretrievable days. *Take* time to enjoy life—to watch a spider construct her web, to play jacks with the girls, to attend a tea party, to watch your Little Leaguer.

Take time to savor the romance of your marriage. Take the time it takes to ooh and ah over the new lawn mower, or the just-made curtains. Make a baked Alaska, or bring home a fistful of violets for an I-love-you surprise.

Time is for listening. It is so easy to tune people out. Like the fellow whose half-listening to a conversation left him suddenly aware that he had been asked a question for which an answer was expected. "I'm sorry," he mumbled apologetically. "My mind was on what I was thinking about."

Ah, so. Us, too. Thinking *our* thoughts, and tuning out the mundane chatter (and the proffered confidences?) of another. We don't *hear* the cloaked cry for help. We don't *hear* the good idea. We don't take time for intentional listening.

"It's just too easy to have appointments or meetings at that peculiar moment when a child needs to unburden his soul—so I'm careful to be home when they are and I try to keep myself really able to hear what they have to say." [1]

It is easy to be too busy, with much ado about everything. We can make them shy off, lest they intrude with their small cares into the Important Projects upon which we happen to be working.

Grandfathers, as well as children, need to be listened to. And so do those who feel that they are so nearly grown. Each has much to say, much that is worthy, if we listen with the expectation of worth. A grandparent has the wisdom of having lived. A child has a wisdom of having freshly seen. A youth has a contemporary wisdom. But all need a sounding board against which to test ideas, and a partner in dialogue.

In listening to these within our own household, in listening to others in the community, in really listening to a newcast, we may find that we are indeed listening to truth.

Savor life as it is. It has built-in problems, but so has every other life in every other age. *This* age is vibrant and creative and revolutionary. What a privilege to be a part of it! Savor it. There is so much of fun and laughter and joy in being a family *now*. Take time to celebrate it. It is for such things as this that we have saved some time.

[1] From "The Three Sons of Levi Smith," Part II. *Life,* December 2, 1966, p. 80.

Money Management

Having agreed that being the world's best consumer is not really the ultimate in life, the family must make certain basic decisions regarding the use of its money.

First, we must get it into perspective. What *are* life's ultimates? Some of them money can buy; some of them it cannot.

As Americans, we seem to have inherited a barely suppressed fear of money. Our forebears spake of it as "filthy lucre," and moralized on the biblical "root of all evil." Conversely, we have an almost obsessive fear of being without it. This later is compounded by life in an over-advertised world of things, most of which can be bought with "no down payment, and the first payment deferred for ninety days." Over-enticed, we soon become over-extended, until we find ourselves over-whelmed. The intentional family will not fall into this trap for the unwary.

When we talk about money and what we do with it, we are not talking *just* about financial resources—we are talking about a total philosophy. What we do with the money we have tells a great deal about the kind of people we are.

Each family reaches some decision about what it wants to do and to be. Money is simply one of the tools it has to get on with that task. It is only practical, then, to plan how best to use it.

111

A budget is such a plan. No two are alike, because no two families are alike. Each has its own set expenses and its own pattern of spending.

A look at past spending patterns will give the family some basis for planning. Keeping a record of what we actually spend over a definite period of time can be extremely revealing. It spots the leaky faucets of family finance, and is a good preliminary study.

That done, we are ready to establish the budget itself. Maybe the best approach is that of a geometry problem:

Given:

        Mary's salary $......
        John's salary $......
        Other income $......

Required: The support of this family in its chosen task.

Solution: The budget.

In setting up the structure, keep the budget streamlined. If it becomes too detailed it will be tiring and self-defeating. Many of the little details can be put into a "slush fund." (Watch it, though. A slush fund is necessary, but it can become engulfing.)

Keep it flexible. The purpose of the budget is to further the family's mission. If, in order to do so, you need to change something, then change it. It is neither against the law nor an admission of defeat to change a plan.

Be honest as you examine your schedule of spending. It is easy to include an item just because it sounds good, or is traditional, or the Joneses do it, or you feel vaguely that perhaps it should be included. The intentional family must examine its expenses with objective honesty.

Having a budget is like taking exercises. We must keep it up if it going to make any difference. Merely putting it down on paper does not alter the condition of the bank account. A budget is to be made, re-examined on occasion, and adhered to.

Few families have enough money to do all the things they would really like to do, or go all the places, or build . . . or buy . . . We must reconcile what we have with what we want to accomplish, and avoid wasting any of it by frittering it away or by spending it on things that we really do not even want.

Things can become an economic tyranny over the family. A house, a boat, a yard—any one of these can become enslaving. Any one of these *can* be an integral part of the family's mission. If so, it should be part of the budget. If not, prune it out ruthlessly. Let us not allow ourselves to become enslaved by things.

A criterion by which we may judge a considered expense is simply this: what does it take to get the job done? If the job—that is, the mission which the family has undertaken—honestly requires a $100 suit, so be it. If it can be done just as well in a $35 copy, buy that one instead.

"I get so frustrated," Marian said. "It takes all we've got to pay the bills—to attend to the necessaries. There is never anything left over to do the good, worthy things we would really *like* to do."

"What are you calling the *necessaries?*"

"Well, two cars. Jim drives his to work every morning. I drive mine in the opposite direction on a different time schedule, to teach. That means insurance, gas, depreciation, car payments . . ."

"Can you do without two cars?"

"No. We must have them both."

"All right. That decision is made; they are necessary. You do whatever is required to get the job done. Two cars are required. Don't waste time fretting about it, but move on to something else."

So. We evaluate, establish priorities—and devise a comprehensive plan.

Once upon a time there *wasn't* any money. It was invented by man as a convenience, to simplify the marketing. We err when we allow it to become a god. That is what we make of it when we orient our whole lives around it.

Money has no value of itself. It is important only for what we can do with it.

THE FAMILY IN THE WORLD

The function of the budget is to bring relative order into the economic aspects of family life, from the point of view of its self-understanding. The perspective is that of the Family in Mission in and to the human enterprise of civilization.

The Family Responsibility to the Family	The Family Responsibility to the World

The Physical Maintenance of the Family

1. Housing	2. Utilities	3. Food	4. Health

The Social Development of the Family

1. Personal appearance	2. Home decor	3. Education provision	4. Transportation

The Family Identity

1. Celebration	2. Recreation	3. Vacations	4. Allowances

The Economic Stability of Society

1. Life insurance	2. Other insurance tools	3. Vocational tools	4. Investment Savings

The Political Security of Society

1. Income taxes	2. Property taxes	3. Misc. taxes	4. Automobile taxes

The Cultural Effectiveness of Society

1. Church benevolence	2. Social benevolence	3. Family-initiated altruism	4. Cash savings

Adapted from materials of the Ecumenical Institute, Chicago, Ill.

Management of Resources

The intentional family has a real responsibility both to proclaim and to practice responsible stewardship of the planet Earth.

We, the family, appreciate the conveniences of modern packaging. But we, humankind, are paying too great a price for that convenience. Statisticians say that the average American family annually throws into the trash *one ton* of packaging materials. That is to say, each year we have paid for, brought home, removed, and thrown away one ton of paper and plastic which must be burned (adding that much *permanent* pollutant to the atmosphere) or dumped, taking up that much of the limited space on the earth's surface. There are specific things that can be done to decrease a family's annual trash pile.

It is not necessary to use one sack for the three onions I purchase at the supermarket, and another for the apples, and still another for the tomatoes. I can simply put the produce in the grocery cart, and carry it all out of the store in one big bag. When the six pork chops and the two pounds of hamburger I wish to purchase are attractively displayed in pretty styrofoam trays, I can *question*. If unpackaged meat is available, I can simply ask the butcher not to wrap mine with a tray, "in the interest of ecology." Or I can write the store manager, and/or the home office, requesting their *serious* consideration of the problem. It is their problem, too. It is everybody's problem. And it needs to be called to our common attention repeatedly.

When I'm checking out at the dime store, and I've only purchased a roll of tape, I can decline the sack, "because we are trying to cut down on our ton of waste packaging this year."

I can make cloth napkins, quickly stitched up from gay no-iron prints, and dispense with the three-times-a-day disposal of wadded-up paper ones. (Cloth napkins needn't be washed after every meal, either! Simple, attractive napkin holders keep them identified, and give a bonus party-place-card atmosphere to the table.)

We can avoid the purchase of soft drinks in nonreturnable bottles and cans. And we can write the manufacturers, today, that we consider their "convenience packaging" a disservice to the nation. Companies *listen* to customers, and we have something to say.

Packaging, of course, is only a portion of the trash we throw out. And the trash is only a portion of the pollution problem. But there are things—specific things—which the concerned family can do. Here are some cases in point:

(1) Keep the car tuned up. Excessive exhaust is an obvious pollutant.

(2) Install anti-smog devices on cars. Support legislation that *requires* it.

(3) Use the car less. Some families have *intentionally* sold their cars.

(4) Purchase biodegradable detergents, for both laundry and dishes. These will break down chemically, and therefore will not contribute to the horrible pollution of river water.

(5) Write legislators regarding current anti-pollution matters.

(6) Speak up on local levels, requiring an accounting of *this* community regarding its own pollution problems.

(7) Write factories or institutions whose chimneys pour pollutants into the air, asking whether or not they have already made plans to correct the problem, and when these plans are to be implemented. People *will* listen, if enough of us express our common concern for this worldwide problem. Gross violators *need* to be called to account.

(8) Write anti-pollution agencies, expressing our concern and asking how best to participate.

These are *little* things that we can do, and we have an imperative obligation to *do* them.

But let us not lull ourselves into complacency just because we've quit buying paper napkins. The problem is world wide and gargantuan. Steps to solve it must also be worldwide and gargantuan.

Seventy percent of the earth's oxygen comes from the phytoplankton in the oceans. We are dumping one million tons of oil pollutants into the world's oceans every year. And the oil obliterates the plankton. How long can we continue practices of this sort? How can the intentional family *not* cry out for action? The U.S. alone releases 142 million tons of pollutants into the air annually. (We have 8 percent of the world's population, and contribute 32 per cent of the world's pollution.)

There *are* solutions. In Japan, there are successful pilot projects in which highly compressed trash has been made into blocks from which houses are being constructed. At Texas A. & M. successful experiments have been carried out using ground glass as an aggregate in paving. Eighty percent of all the copper ever mined is still in circulation because we reclaim it. In Los Angeles an aluminum company test project has got people to redeem a million aluminum cans a month! And they are about to introduce the project in sixteen states.

Things can be done. The answers are neither easy nor cheap. But the alternative is annihilation.

Chapter Eight

The Family Faces Change

The family of today finds itself in the midst of unprecedented and universal revolution.

We no longer have a nice pat set of rules by which to live.

No wonder we are confused.

No wonder we find ourselves floundering in uncertainty.

It is not ours to decide whether or not we shall be a part of this upheaval; it has tumbled in upon us.

The choices we do have are whether we as a family shall try to ignore change, drag our feet and protest it, or pick up our destiny and help shape the future. The first choice is unreal; the second is its own damnation. The third choice is the intentional family's only available option.

Some of the changes thrust upon us are worldwide. We are in the midst of an information explosion. More books have been written in the past fifteen years than in all previous years of history.

More facts have been accumulated and classified. Dr. Mortimer Adler has stated that the available information now doubles about every eight and a half years.[1]

We are part of a new technology. Ninety-five percent of all the scientists who ever lived are alive and working today. Technical know-how is a key resource.

The population explosion threatens us all. Twenty-five percent of all the people who ever lived are alive today. In 650 years (at the present rate of world population growth) there will be one square foot of land for each person on earth. Population equaling a city the size of Chicago is added every month. In the metropolitan areas of Los Angeles and New York, the population has increased 700 persons per day for the last ten years.

Is this any longer a situation which we can ignore? Can we help our children think through this problem? Is it any longer *moral* to consider raising a big family? What is our political moral obligation here? maybe

In the past, being intentional about the size of the family meant not having more children than the parents could support financially. But we are part of the family of man, and we are *already* more than we can support.

The rural mind-set of yesterday is being re-

[1] *Today* show, February 27, 1969.

121

placed by the urban orientation of today. The intimate and the provincial have given way to the anonymous and the comprehensive. The little cottage with the white picket fence has given way to the high-rise apartment dwelling, and the corner grocery to the impersonal supermarket.

The current political revolution calls for the assumption of new responsibility on the part of both candidates and voters. Grandad was born a Democrat and died a Democrat. Today, to the vast confusion of both major parties, many people feel free to vote by their current decision.

A cultural revolution sweeps the world. There is an awakening consciousness of all minority groups. Prescribed roles of the past are being cast off. We no longer feel obliged to accept anything, just because that's the way it was always done, or said, or adhered to.

The generation gap is increasingly frustrating. Half the world's population is under twenty-four years of age. With the continued developments of medical science, more people live longer than ever before. And communication difficulties are compounded.

Pollution is a growing menace. "The Family of Man, traveling together on the spaceship Earth, has a limited supply of air, water, soil. We are preserved from annihilation only by the care . . . we give our fragile craft." [2]

[2] Adlai Stevenson's final speech.

These are all changes, drastic and basic changes, that will increasingly affect the way we think and live. That the family faces change is a foregone conclusion. *How* we face these and other changes can be a matter of intention.

Sometimes change comes in the nature of a local family crisis. It may be instigated from within the family, or it may come suddenly and without warning from the outside. In either case, the family will face the decision (if there is one to be made) or accept the inevitable—and then move out from the present crisis to get on with the task.

Moving

There was a time when a child was born in the house his grandfather built. He grew up in that house, brought his bride there, raised his children and indulged his grandchildren, all in that same house.

Now the average American family moves every four years. Moves! Packs up all its earthly possessions and changes its address! It pulls up its roots, and plants them again elsewhere.

Often families who move have a choice as to what this will do to them: They can decide to cling to one another for support and security, to the exclusion of other relationships in each new community; or they can decide to *plant* their roots again elsewhere, getting acquainted and becoming active participants in each new community. Those who choose to address themselves only to one another may have the pleasure of hearing others say, "What a *close* family"—when the truth of the matter may be that they have become ingrown. A family self-centeredness can become as selfish as personal self-centeredness. Togetherness is good; but this exclusive togetherness is not the goal of the intentional family.

On the other hand, the family who moves often finds expanded horizons and increased opportunities to fulfill its mission. It can intentionally infiltrate all manner of communities and organizations and situations.

> (And besides,
> a rolling stone gathers no moss,
> but gains a highly burnished gloss
> that rarely ever can be found
> on rocks imbedded in the ground.)

Sometimes the family has on opportunity to decide, intentionally, whether or not this move is one to make. If it is going to hurt the family, or undermine its mission, then an increase in salary does not make it valid. If, however, this move is advisable, even a *decrease* in salary should not halt it. And the family sets about its relocation deliberately, packing what is useful and discarding what is outgrown. This can be done both actually and symbolically. We can, for instance, discard our prejudices and pack up our possibilities in a ritual that sends us out to be the Family for Others in a new situation.

Changing Jobs

Recent statistics state that the average American man changes careers three times. Not just *jobs—careers.* We are also told that the technological man is obsolete in five years, unless he participates in some sort of continuing education process.

This means a number of things to the intentional family. One may be that it must enable the breadwinner to go back to school, or to take industrial updating courses from time to time.

For another, it is now required that we sit a little looser in the saddle—that we be freer and more flexible than in years past, and that we feel less threatened by change.

It means also that we are less bound by vocational ties than families once were. It is now *possible* to change careers, and to make a go of it. Other people are managing to do it. If the job that I am in is one in which I am a miserable misfit, or one which cannot in any sense be used to further my mission, I can at least be open to the possibility of choosing another.

The intentional family will help guide its youth in the matter of choosing careers. A number of tests are now available that analyze skills and abilities, and that are even able to ascertain interests with reasonable accuracy. Many of these are given as part of the counseling programs in junior high and senior high schools. They are indicative and helpful, but they are not always enough. Can we help further by exposing our children to all sorts of careers, that they may better understand the available options? The old adage to "learn something about everything you can, and everything you can about a selective something" is of particular pertinence here. The youngster who knows nothing but dairy farming may be singularly inept at that—but he chooses it as a career because he can't think of any other one.

Sometimes we offer youngsters a valuable service by helping them project to its logical conclusion a proposed career based on an absorbing interest. Carol loved music and was an accomplished cellist. It seemed to her a logical choice for a career. An intentional interview with a professional musician changed her plans, however. In her part of the country, the only full-time career openings in music are for school band directors.

An interview with a professional in his field of endeavor, some boning up at the library, a discussion with officials at an employment office, can help a young person make an intelligent initial choice.

It is possible to follow up on a definitive aptitude test. What jobs are there along these lines that I did not even know about? Do any of them sound intriguing? More, do any of them sound as though they might be done on behalf of all mankind? Anything less is not sufficiently challenging to choose as a career.

Some are lucky enough to have jobs that are a vocation. Some jobs are carried on simply because they give one the income to live on while he carries out his real vocation.

By way of deliberate digression, we may need to follow up on *other* sorts of tests given to our children at school. Or we may need to seek out, through a community mental health service, the assistance of a testing and diagnostic program for any member of the family. In a push-pull, tension-filled world, mental disturbances are a real possibility for parents or children.

Measles has an identifiable rash. A strep throat has its own unique symptoms. Unfortunately, mental disturbance does not come with labels so easy to read. We are so sure that it can't happen to us that we blind ourselves to symptoms and deafen our ears to that cloaked cry for help. Prolonged maladjustment, however, or deep depression, or markedly inconsistent behavior of any member of the family should move us to request help. One American out of every ten has or will have mental illness. It should bear no more stigma than a physical ailment. Either requires professional help.

Accepting a child as he is, does not mean ignoring symptoms of a growing neurosis or flagrant behavior deviations.

Leisure Time

America has not yet really adjusted to the forty-hour work week. But the knowledgeable ones are predicting that by the year 2000, less than three short decades away, we will have a *thirteen*-hour work week. How then shall the family cope with its leisure time?

Already we pursue recreation with such competitive intensity that it becomes more exhausting than work.

A man is not required to hunt or fish. Or play golf. These are aceptable forms of recreation only to those who find them recreational. But when they become a way of life. . .

A housewife plays bridge with total dedication if that is all she has. But if life is intentional, and there are tasks that claim her devotion, then playing bridge falls into a more reasonable perspective.

Leisure time? What is it, anyway? By definition, the word refers to that time left over after one has fulfilled his obligations of employment. The obligations of employment, though, are not the *only* obligations to which we are subject. What about our obligations to the political community? the school district? the local church? our own family? the community?

Thank goodness for leisure time—which makes possible our participation in all these.

The change in working hours is making available greater segments of leisure. Work days are shorter. Weekends are longer. Vacations are longer. Retirement comes earlier. ("Tapering-off retirement" beginning at 45 to 50 is already a part of some organization employment plans.)

Great! These new segments of time increase the possibilities for the intentional family. More and more things become possible as time becomes available. *Employment* is often a working-for-ourselves; *leisure time* enables a working-for-others to a degree that has not been possible before. Almost without thinking, we fall into a habit of regarding the hind part before. "I work all day for the boss; by gum, my time off is gonna be for me." This is not really true. I work all day or all week to earn the paycheck that is mine to spend. That is unquestionably for me. A portion of my leisure time should be invested on behalf of others.

The intentional family seizes with delight the extra bonuses of time that a changing society decrees.

Divorce

The family has always been the basic unit of society. If it breaks up, it affects the whole of society.

Changing mores, however, have made divorce a more and more common occurrence. Today there are really very few families who have not been touched in some relationship by divorce.

Marriages seldom fail. Relationships that pass for marriage frequently do. A couple has actually failed to achieve a marriage when their relationship is not strong enough to survive the stresses of mutual adjustment and individual differences.

There are circumstances in which divorce is the lesser of two evils: and "the continuance of the marriage may cause greater damage to the personalities involved and greater insecurity for the children than its termination." [3]

That being so, there is no feasible alternative to divorce. The decision is never one to be made hastily, or in anger or spite. But if, after considerable soul-searching, and after an intensive series

[3] James Pike, *Doing the Truth*, p. 146.

of conferences with a trained marriage counselor and an understanding minister, such a decision is made—then it is made. The intentional family moves on from that point. There is no time for dwelling on "if onlys." The business of living requires their attention.

One portion of life is ended. Another begins. An intentional family seizes this new beginning and makes the necessary decisions to shape its future. Careful planning—establishing comprehensive goals and the right-now implementation —is required.

It is a good time to paint the house, perhaps, or to plant a couple of rose bushes out front. These are graphic ways of saying to themselves and to the world at large, "We live here! A *family* still dwells at this address." Whether or not the family has a front yard in which to speak its piece, there are other less obvious ways in which it expresses even more significantly the ongoingness of the family unit.

It is a good time also to take a greater responsibility in and for the community.

Growing Older

In the beginning, we were two, and life was wonderfully exciting and romantic and full. Then the babies came along, and we had all we could do just getting the diapers folded and the bottles filled. We were enthralled—thrilled and excited with a first smile and a first word and a first step. Babies are so sweet-smelling and soft, their hair so silky, their hands so unbelievably small with tiny fingers that wrap themselves around a parental thumb (and heart) and won't let go. Toddlers are so bewitching—so eager to learn and so eager to please. Pre-schoolers are so fun to watch, developing their own personalities, experimenting in independence.

And all this time, the parents are increasingly engrossed in the children. Because they are so dependent upon us, we have wrapped up our whole lives in providing for them. "There isn't the time. . ." "There isn't the money. . ." There really isn't the *interest* in working at any personal growth.

The growing children begin to get involved in school and music lessons and baseball and scout troops, and we find their lives even more exciting. If anything, we are busier, providing an afternoon snack, hauling them here and there, attending this, helping with that—until suddenly they are in college. Now the things they are doing and learning are even more engrossing. Their continued (and increased) financial dependence requires our complete concentration. They are still the hub around which we revolve. We are still necessary to them, and completely involved with them.

And then . . . Quite suddenly they are gone.

Graduated, with jobs of their own, they no longer *need* us financially. Married, with families of their own, they no longer *need* us emotionally.

And we are bereft. Because we have not had any existence outside the lives of our children, we are bereft.

Unless, of course, we have faced this moment from the time we took the marriage vows. We have known all along that it would come. If we have prepared for it intentionally, and with periodic re-evaluation, then it comes as a change fraught with all sorts of new opportunities.

Now we can *really* get involved in the League of Women Voters. Now we can *serve* on the Chamber of Commerce, with the time to do it effectively, and to use our membership therein intentionally.

There may be ten more years of active employment before retirement age. These are choice years. Income is still high, but expenses are less. There can be a new freedom in the spending—a new fun in being *able* to do and to give. "You don't have to be a millionaire," she tried to explain "to have an awful lot of fun. And you don't have to be rich to be a philanthropist." What choice years indeed, if they are faced beforehand and entered into intentionally.

Retirement

That is the last straw for the unintentional.

No longer needed on the job, they feel no longer needed anywhere. And to be no longer needed is degrading. It lessens one's opinion of himself.

Retirement has come. Now there is nothing left. Unless we have had something on the back burner we've had it. Unless . . .

Retirement? Whoopee! *Now* we can join the Peace Corps. Or Vista. Now we can move into that situation at "Pig City" and really get some things done. *Now* we can take on a menial task at the rehabilitation center, and simply *be* there, *present* to people who need people.

Now, at this point in life, we have the time *and* the wisdom to do some lucid thinking and some therefore valid service on behalf of all mankind.

Death

There are some situations in which a person longs for death. This is rare, though. Most of us really just don't want to die. We do not want to anticipate it—or even to give practical consideration to how we as a family shall meet it.

It is possible to be as intentional about facing death as we try to be about facing life. But in order to do so, we must do our homework here, too.

First, we need to get it into perspective.

Death is.

Our unwillingness to admit it does not make it any less so. It will happen, even to those we love—even to us.

Second, there are some practical approaches that we can make to this common experience.

1. We need to make a will.

2. We need to get our affairs in order, with pertinent papers and documents and policies in the same place. Someone outside the family needs to know where these things are kept.

These are things that most families make some effort to attend to.

The intentional family will go a step further, making provision for the future of the children. What will happen to them if both parents should die? Discussing it now enables us to make definite plans. With whom would they live? Is that family willing to take them in? What can we do to provide for them financially? These plans need to be made in some detail, then updated periodically.

What if the father dies? Would insurance cover a period of time during which the mother could finish schooling, that she might then assume part of the financial load? If the mother dies first, what plans can be made ahead of time in regard to the children? Plans in some detail should be made for the family as a whole. Maybe there is no financial burden. Then the plan could include volunteer work for the surviving parent, in an area that has long been of interest. Doing volunteer work just to get out of the house is no help. But active participation in something that matters can give *reason* to life!

"We should talk this over, but it is so hard to talk about now." Hard to talk about? Not if we have accepted death as another part of life, about which we can also be intentional. It is certainly easier for two to make intelligent decisions on a calm and ordinary day, than for one to be faced with them alone in a moment of grief.

The intentional person may make certain advance decisions about his own death. If he intends to leave his eyes to an eye bank to give sight to others, there are legal forms to be filled out, and someone else needs to know of the intention.

What about the "trappings" of death? Would I prefer a $3,000 casket, or perhaps a simpler one for a third of that, with the balance invested in lives? Will my reticence to say so now cause my family, in their moment of uncertainty, to invest in trappings that are a financial jeopardy to their own future?

There are other more important decisions which we as intentional people need to make about death. They concern attitudes.

I have but one death. How shall I use it?

Ike Edwards' work might come under the title of *reconciliation*. It requires that he travel a great deal. Most of this he does by plane. He is aware and his wife is aware each time he leaves that he may not make it back. But they have decided that the work he does is so important that even if he gives his life in it, it is all right.

Is the work that I do that important? If I had nine deaths to use, I could waste one or two without it mattering a great deal. But I have only this one, and it behooves me to give some serious thought as to how I shall spend it.

Death brings change to the family. Sometimes the death is sudden and unexpected. Even then it will be easier to accept if a rational attitude has been established. So let us *discuss* death, without hesitation. Let us *admit* that Aunt Edna is critically ill, and that death may be very near for her. Let us mention that the astronauts whom our children admire seem to face their risk quite calmly. We do the children a disservice when we continually skirt the issue. We deny all of us the strength that we can gain from one another in times of sorrow. How shall they come to an understanding of death except through these experiences? Does our attitude witness to Christian faith, or to some semi-pagan fear?

How *shall* they come to an understanding of death? Through watching Mama's soap opera, or reading *Little Women,* or through participation in a family's acceptance of a natural part of life?

The intentional family may need to celebrate a death through ritual. Talking together about "what kind of man he was, what sort of life he lived, what he wanted us to be," is a sort of ritual. It is a reminder of how he lived, and a sending us out on his behalf. This moment, while our hearts are still tender, is one in which we can see our own humanness most fully. Now, while our hearts are still tender, death places a demand upon us to look at our own lives and see whether or not they are worthwhile.

Chapter Nine

Life-Style

Each family, in its own moment of truth, must choose what its life-style shall be. It can decide to be intentional, undertaking on behalf of all mankind. Or it can decide that such undertaking is not worth what it will cost—that it is "too much bother"—and that it is more sensible to live only for itself. Intentional? Or otherwise? *Each* family decides.

And not to decide is merely another way of deciding.

Psychologist Erich Fromm spoke of the two alternatives as man-for-himself and man-for-others.[1] The first life-style he terms "non-productive," and sees it characterized by receiving, exploiting, hoarding, and marketing; the second is "productive," characterized by care, responsibility, respect, and knowledge. When we translate his list of personality traits into the vernacular, we see both attitudes within ourselves.

[1] Erich Fromm, *Man for Himself* (New York: Holt, Rinehart & Winston, 1947), pp. 98-101.

Non-Productive		Productive	
Fromm	Vernacular	Fromm	Vernacular
Receptivity	"Gimme"	Care	"I am willing to work for your good."
Exploitation	"How can I use you?"	Responsi-bility	"Your burden is my burden."
Hoarding	"I'll keep what I've got."	Respect	"I accept you as you are."
Marketing	"What can I get out of this?"	Knowledge	"I can't help at all without first doing my home-work."

What we are choosing is not a simple alternative for a specific occasion but a way of life—a *style* of life. This is the basic decision, from which all others are made.

For some, the decision is made outside the frame of reference of the Christian faith. For others, it is conceivable only as it *implements* Christian faith. Certainly an honest appraisal of biblical history leads us to this same decision of whether to be a man-for-self or a man-for-others. The imperative to decide comes to every person in the light of the best that he knows. Within *any* frame of reference, the understanding of some will be more comprehensive, more aware, than the understanding of others.

We can set out to accomplish the necessary deed as humanists, doing what we do simply for the good of mankind. Or we can do the necessary deed in response to God's love. Our concern for others must be not a stand-off-and-think-sweet-thoughts kind of love, but *agape*—a deeply moving, working, hurting-longing love that expresses itself in the dedicated undertaking of the burdens of the world. It is in this that we find the context for decision.

The decision is not, basically, an emotional one. It is a hard, lucid, clearheaded, self-conscious, and honest-to-God commitment.

The decision to *live* our lives is one that we make individually, but it is also one that we can make more effective if we can put behind it the united efforts of the whole family. *This* family, within *this* household, affirms its *common* decision (and its *un*common dedication) to be the people of God in today's world. Accepting one another as we are, aware of our dependence on and our responsibilities to one another, this family leans into the task with a strength that is *more* than the sum of its members. One member alone cannot be what he has to be, if he is begrudgingly released by the others. But if he is sent out *by* the family and on behalf of the family, he walks with the strength of six—or two—or five. Or ———.

The decision to live intentionally is one made in the light of community and world needs. No family is an island. Each family lives its decision, if it is to be a valid one, in the context of world food crises, and national minority strife, and local school board decisions. It *must* be aware of the needs of the lonely widow across the alley, and the mentally retarded adult who vegetates next door. Then, in this awareness, it must seek out and participate in some ongoing solution to the problem it sees, or initiate one.

The intentional family reaffirms its task in moments of celebration. It reminds its members of their common goals as it seeks to express them in the words of a ritual. It focuses its celebrations on that which is valid, savoring the worthy traditions and establishing new ones. On the occasions which make ritual necessary, it uses the ritual to lend the occasions depth.

The family seizes every opportunity to remind itself of what it is about. It uses the bulletin board, the decor in the living room, the arrangement of the backyard—to express its stance.

Daring to think and requiring itself to study, the family does its homework. Without this it serves ignorantly, which is no service at all. It *enjoys* the study, the stimulation of new ideas. It finds challenge and heady joy in the hard discipline of the focused mind.

The intentional family may implement its task in the family council. It decides to seize its irretrievable days, its gonna-get-spent-somehow money—and puts them both where they'll count! It laughs and gives, and listens and saves, and savors—and spends itself with intentional abandon!

Once the basic decision is made, the family is freed—*we* are freed—to be ourselves, to spend the uniqueness that *is* this family, in a newly significant life for others.

Steeped in the *best* traditions of our faith, we have access to the wisdom and the insight of past men of stature. They give us the possibility of moving beyond anything we could have thought through on our own.

Obliged by this tradition to be revolutionary, we cannot afford to remain placid in this world. We must move out, daringly, in a kind of lucid lunacy—ready, if need be, to give our death in order to create a new future.

This life-style is no discipline in absentmindedness. We must be sharply aware of the times, aware of the people—all people—hearing both what is said and what is left unsaid.

Having heard, we must put our service, unwitholdingly, where it will do the most good.

143

This is going to be work. The old church word *liturgy* is from the Greek, and means *hard, sweaty work.* So be it.

We celebrate our humanness, and we participate with joy in each day's challenge, utterly open to the future—for we have chosen to live.